CHALLENGE-BASED LEARNING IN THE SCHOOL LIBRARY MAKERSPACE

Colleen Graves, Aaron Graves,
and Diana L. Rendina

LIBRARIES
UNLIMITED™
An Imprint of ABC-CLIO, LLC
Santa Barbara, California • Denver, Colorado

Library of Congress Cataloging-in-Publication Data

Names: Graves, Colleen, author. | Graves, Aaron, author. |
    Rendina, Diana L., author.
Title: Challenge-based learning in the school library makerspace /
    Colleen Graves, Aaron Graves, and Diana L. Rendina.
Description: Santa Barbara, California : Libraries Unlimited,
    an imprint of ABC-CLIO, LLC, [2017] | Includes bibliographical
    references and index.
Identifiers: LCCN 2017018676 (print) | LCCN 2017003518 (ebook) |
    ISBN 9781440851513 (ebook) | ISBN 9781440851506
    (paperback : acid-free paper)
Subjects: LCSH: School libraries—Activity programs. | Makerspaces
    in libraries. | Maker movement in education.
Classification: LCC Z675.S3 (print) | LCC Z675.S3 G677 2017 (ebook) |
    DDC 027.8—dc23
LC record available at https://lccn.loc.gov/2017018676

ISBN: 978-1-4408-5150-6
EISBN: 978-1-4408-5151-3

21 20 19 18 17   1 2 3 4 5

This book is also available as an eBook.

Libraries Unlimited
An Imprint of ABC-CLIO, LLC

ABC-CLIO, LLC
130 Cremona Drive, P.O. Box 1911
Santa Barbara, California 93116-1911
www.abc-clio.com

This book is printed on acid-free paper (∞)

Manufactured in the United States of America

Contents

Preface

Diana Rendina was the media specialist at Stewart Middle Magnet School in Tampa, Florida, from 2010 to 2017. Stewart is a public, Title 1 STEM magnet school located near downtown Tampa. Diana wanted to find a way to connect the school's STEM magnet theme with her library program. In late 2013, she learned about the Maker Movement in education and began reading everything she could find. She shared her vision with anyone who would listen and eventually acquired several bins of K'nex that had been used by the science department in the past. She cleaned off the dust, put them out on the library tables, and, in January 2014, her makerspace was born. Her maker program continued to grow and expand and is now a vital part of the library. Students come and use the makerspace throughout the school day, during school STEAM club, and at the afterschool Stewart Makers Club. Diana is now the media specialist at Tampa Prepartory School, a 6–12 independent school.

Colleen Graves is a teacher librarian who wears many hats. As a longtime English teacher turned librarian, she values making, writing, and bringing creative education into all school subjects. As soon as she started working in her own library, she knew she wanted to incorporate maker education. What started as an afterschool month-long club became a way of daily education. Throughout the book, Colleen writes about her journey in incorporating making into an affluent middle school and into a lower socioeconomic high school.

Aaron Graves is a public school librarian at Denton High School in Denton, Texas. After moving to the campus in 2015, Aaron started to look for ways to incorporate making and breathe new life into the traditional library program. Denton High School is an International Baccalaureate School, which makes it a natural fit for makerspaces. It allows students to pursue their research and design aspirations, which the International Baccalaureate curriculum fosters.

One of his greatest passions is incorporating making and physical application of abstract concepts into learning experiences for students.

Throughout the book, the authors are referenced to explain how making, design, and challenge-based learning took root in our libraries. In some instances, the authors collaborated on design challenges and piggy backed off one another's ideas to cultivate a creative space in each library. We hope you see steps in our journey that can springboard your library into your own maker journey.

1

Participatory Learning in a Makerspace

Immerse your students in maker supplies. Just as surrounding kids with books motivates them to read, surrounding them with tinkering tools motivates them to create. You don't need a special room for your makerspace. All you need are maker resources, somewhere to store items, and a beginner's knowledge of how to use your resources.
—Colleen Graves (2015, blog)

WHAT IS A MAKERSPACE?

A makerspace is not a room. It's a concept. The library is the "maker" space because it is the "space" where "makers" create. According to the *Makerspace Playbook*: "Makerspaces come in all shapes and sizes, but they all serve as a gathering point for tools, projects, mentors and expertise. A collection of tools does not define a space; rather, we define it by what it enables: making" (The Makerspace Team 2013). Makerspaces are about providing tools and materials to encourage a maker mind-set focused on creativity. There is no such thing as a "one-size-fits-all" makerspace—it is about creating a space and environment that works best for each school. Educators can create amazing makerspaces in schools whether the budget is $10,000 or $0. Meaningful participatory learning experiences can be created for students with a stack of cardboard and tape, a bin full of LEGOs, or electronic circuit kits.

Makerspaces can be anywhere in the school, and a school can have more than one. They're fantastic in classrooms, in open common spaces, and, of course, in libraries. We feel that the library is an ideal location in schools for makerspaces. One of the central tenets of school libraries is to make resources and tools accessible to *all* students—whether they are gifted or repeating the year and whether they are from affluent families or of a lower socioeconomic status. Makerspaces provide resources and tools that students can use for both class projects and personal exploration, and libraries are an ideal location for these resources and tools. Libraries are the great equalizer of schools and are available to the entire school population regardless of their class schedules and interests. Students don't have to depend on a specific teacher bringing them to the makerspace to participate when it's in the library because the space is available to all classes and students. With all of this in mind, it makes perfect sense to incorporate makerspaces into school libraries, and there are many different ways to integrate this creative programming.

In the beginning, Colleen, as a librarian at Lamar Middle School, separated her makerspace supplies from the main library and tried to create a separate room for students where they could make things. Students did not utilize the space the way she thought they would, and all of the maker programming was held in the main library space anyway. What was the purpose of storing things in another room other than to lock it up?

So she moved the makerspace materials at Lamar Middle School into an easily accessible area behind the circulation desk and instituted a project shelf. What happened? Her students started tinkering every day! The materials were accessible, but more expensive items were still safely located further behind the desk. Students could easily grab maker resources from colorful tubs and start creating. The placement of the tools doesn't matter. What matters is having accessible tools and teaching students to tinker to learn. In "Designing for Tinkerability," Resnick and Rosenbaum describe this method of learning and how it not only engages students but also helps them create new ideas. The approach is more important than the stuff as you can see in their description: "The tinkering approach is characterized by a playful, experimental, iterative style of engagement, in which makers are continually reassessing their goals, exploring new paths, and imagining new possibilities" (Resnick and Rosenbaum 2013, 164). No matter where you keep items, making and tinkering are important learning techniques in the library makerspace because this approach prepares our students for the future. According to Resnick and Rosenbaum,

> We live in a world that is characterized by uncertainty and rapid change. Many of the things you learn today will soon be obsolete. Success in the future will depend not on what you know, or how much you know, but on your ability to think and act creatively—on your ability to come up with innovative solutions to unexpected situations and unanticipated problems. In such a fast-changing environment, tinkering is a particularly valuable strategy. Tinkerers understand how to improvise, adapt, and iterate, so they are never stuck on old plans as new situations arise. Tinkering prioritizes creativity and agility over efficiency and optimization, a worthwhile tradeoff for a constantly changing world. (2013, 166)

Mind-Set over Physical Space

Without a dedicated room or area in the library, it is still possible to incorporate making into a school library. The space itself isn't important. Changing the school's mind-set for learning and the school's openness to play and tinkering are what will create an effective makerspace. Many librarians have converted old book carts into mobile makerspaces that can be stored when not in use. Others have created mini-makerspaces throughout the library like centers or stations. A makerspace does not have to start with a huge commitment. At Stewart Middle Magnet School, media specialist Diana Rendina started the initial makerspace by pushing a couple of library tables together and laying out some bins of K'nex. At Lamar, the first year featured all free or low-cost makerspace activities. The important thing is just to get started creating and building a maker culture and community in the school.

> **Every environment is different. What will create a sustaining makerspace is different for every space. There is a delicate balance between giving help, sharing the lessons learned and inspiring others, but still leaving room for educators to figure it out own their own and making it meaningful for you as the learner.**
> **—Ryan Jenkins, Tinkering Studio Education Developer[1]**

Participatory Learning and Maker Culture

When creating a makerspace and implementing challenge-based learning, it's important to look at the big picture. Many schools have rushed to start makerspaces without spending any time building a maker community in their school. Schools often lack significant participatory learning experiences for students, so the style of learning that is experienced in makerspaces may be a bit of a culture shock. That is why building up a maker community and culture within the school first and foremost is so critical. It is also essential to connect the school makerspace with the local maker community and global maker community. This helps students see beyond the classroom walls and learn that they are part of a greater maker movement.

In her book, *The Participatory Museum*, Nina Simon describes the value of participatory learning experiences and how to create them. While her book is primarily focused on museums, the concepts can be stretched to all cultural institutions, including schools and libraries. Simon describes a participatory cultural institution as "a place where visitors can create, share, and connect with each other around content" (Simon 2010, ii). This concept fits in perfectly with school library makerspaces, as a school makerspace is a space where students create things, whether with cardboard, LEGOs, 3D printers, or other materials. Plus, these makerspaces provide a place where students can share handmade creations and fosters an environment where students can connect with others.

In a makerspace environment, students comfortably and instantaneously snap between the role as a student to a new to role as an expert. Massachusetts Institute of Technology (MIT) professor Neil Gershenfeld identified his students' passion for this role reversal:

---

1. Unless otherwise cited, this and all subsequent Ryan Jenkins quotes are from a telephone interview by the author on July 22, 2016.

Once students mastered a new capability, such as waterjet cutting or microcontroller programming, they had a near-evangelical interest in showing others how to use it. As students needed new skills for their projects, they would learn them from their peers and then in turn pass them on. . . . This process can be thought of as a "just-in-time" educational model, teaching on demand, rather than the more traditional "just -in-case" model. (2005, 7)

Gershenfeld identified this just in time educational model when he realized that students in his experimental class, How to Make (Almost) Anything, were picking up learning as needed. Instead of following a curriculum, "the learning process was driven by the demand for, rather than the supply of knowledge" (Gershenfeld 2005, 7).

When creating a makerspace, it is pertinent to create spaces where students can be "cultural participants, not passive consumers" (Simon 2010, ii). A natural phenomena will occur when students become actively engaged in their learning. Students become empowered by gaining a new skill and then instantly turn around to teach it to someone else. One of Colleen's Ryan High School students was talking about this phenomenon and said, "It might seem awkward at first, but then you realize you can come to the library to make stuff, mess around, and ask other students to help you make something."

CREATING A MAKER COMMUNITY IN YOUR SCHOOL

To foster actively creative students in a successful maker environment, the first step is to cultivate a maker community within the school. The community is already there, you just have to uncover it. As the space starts to grow, students will come out of the woodwork with an interest in making. Students will uncover undiscovered passions and soon identify as coders, robotics enthusiasts, budding engineers, painters, knitters, and more. Sometimes, they'll be the quirky loners; other times, they'll have a diverse group of friends. Connect with these students quickly and find ways to gather them all together—they will be vital in creating a maker community in your school. Starting a maker programming advisory committee is a great place to start. This will give you an idea of what maker students are already doing and interested in learning. Get as many teachers as possible on board to implement a school-wide change.

Form a Maker Steering Committee

It's essential to allow for student voice when planning a makerspace. This space is first and foremost for students, and if it is filled with activities and materials they aren't the least bit interested in, there will be a big problem. Gather interested students and teachers to form a Maker Steering Committee. Let the students brainstorm workshop ideas, perform storage and space planning, and teach other students about making.

Inclusive Strategies

When forming a Maker Steering Committee, make sure to include a representative sampling of the student body. Be intentional about including female students, minorities, students with low socioeconomic status, and other groups present in the school.

Meet with the student committee and share different ideas and activities with them. Print out pictures of different spaces and activities, and let them vote on their favorites by using colored dot stickers. Buy or borrow a few potential maker materials for the space, and let the student committee be the guinea pigs. Be an anthropologist and observe how they interact with different materials and activities. Which materials seem more for fun, and which materials would have a long-term educational use? All of this will be vital in helping plan out the space.

Forming Goals

After you've got your steering committee, work on goal-setting for your makerspace. Make sure your goals address these issues:

- What do you want kids to take away from makerspace activities?
- What do you want kids to learn?
- What skill set do students need that they don't get in a typical classroom?
- How can a maker community support the classroom curriculum and school community?
- Evaluate funding options. What can you get for free, what will you have to budget?
- What items would be best for crowdsourced funding or writing a grant?
- What does the school already have? Are you a 1:1 technology campus where every student is given a device, or is your technology outdated? Is there a wood shop or a science, technology, engineering, and mathematics (STEM) lab already? What will your space provide that's currently lacking in the school?

Establish a Culture of Creativity

What is at the core of your school's culture? What about the culture of your library? Do your mission and vision statements reflect the importance of creativity in your space? Work toward creating an environment of respect and rapport that encourages students to take risks and be creative. Consider rewriting your mission and vision statements to include an emphasis on creative learning, and then post them around the library. The mission statement of the

Stewart Middle Magnet Media Center is "to discover, learn, grow, create, connect, collaborate and explore our world." This short, succinct mission statement helps to put the importance of maker culture within the library front and center. Similarly, the vision statement for Stewart is "We grow dreamers, develop innovators, strengthen critical thinkers, build strong communicators and nourish creative souls who will go out and make the world better for all of us." When students, parents, and community members read these mission and vision statements posted throughout the space, it becomes clear that a culture of creativity is valued.

According to the Ryan High School website, "the vision for the library is to create a safe and inviting environment for students and staff where students and teachers feel comfortable to create, innovate, and collaborate." Colleen incorporates staff into her vision for the space as a way to welcome making and curriculum connections. Her goals for the library programming are to "develop a maker culture where students understand the design thinking process." Her goal in instructional partnerships with teachers is to "empower students to make, create, and become the innovators of the future."

Take some time to work on your mission and vision statements. Make sure that the importance of a culture of creativity is clear and at the forefront in both.

Develop Creativity Stations

Find ways to weave creativity throughout the library by creating mini-makerspaces in the form of creativity stations. These types of stations often focus on a small, quick activity that can get creative juices flowing and encourage a culture of discovery and wonder.

The Participatory Museum (Simon 2010) discusses how to create participatory, interactive museum exhibits, and these have much in common with the type of participatory maker stations being considered here. Like museum staff members, librarians are not always able to directly attend to every student that walks through the doors. Consider ways to let students self-direct their learning in these stations. Create relatively low barriers for entry into these activities—make it possible for students to get started and try them out even if they have little to no experience with the activity. Simon (2010) recommends defining clear roles, providing flexible tools, and allowing participants to engage at their own level of commitment. Make it safe for students to observe passively as well—some students will not be ready to jump in right away, but they might be okay with hanging out and watching their friends participate. Let some students lurk while others create. In a library makerspace, some students are leaders, while others just want to be a part of the community. This is okay because in a makerspace, everyone has a part. Eventually the lurkers will move from a stance of watching to a stance of making.

Just as we incorporate constraints and guidelines into large group design challenges, think about constraints that can be set within the maker station activity. Simon advises that "Participants thrive on constraints. . . . Constraints help scaffold creative experiences" (2010, p 22). Too many options can sometimes be overwhelming, causing students to avoid participation at all. Consider creative, purposeful constraints that can help spur student creativity. For example, what if a LEGO maker station had only yellow LEGOs? Or students had to design a phone holder with K'nex using fewer than 20 pieces?

Examples of Creativity Stations for Libraries

- Set a giant coloring poster and some markers out at a table, and invite students to color.
- Start a collaborative poem on a long sheet of paper, and encourage every student that comes in to add a line.
- Incorporate a giant handmade loom where students can collaboratively make an upcycled rug out of old T-shirts.
- Create a DIY bookmark station where students can design their own bookmark to take home.
- Create "half-baked prototypes" (Jenkins) that invite students to tinker and play with materials. You could create your own #LEGOtinkering musical exploration centers like you would find at the Tinkering Studio in San Francisco's Exploratorium.
- Visit science museums to see exhibits that draw patrons in and encourage them to create and linger. Because museum educators know people are only going to be visiting for a short time, they are great at developing short, participatory projects that have an easy entry point for learners of all ages.
- Create a marble run or movable and changeable marble wall where students can tinker with physics.
- Start a collaborative musical Makey Makey wall, and let students experiment with what is conductive and nonconductive. (See the full plan here at http://makeymakey.com/lessons/interactive-room-challenge.)

While these may all seem like little things, adding these interactive, participatory experiences into the library will help students see that this is a place where creativity is encouraged and valued. Soon students will come in droves to create and add to the participatory culture in your library.

In Chapter 3, we'll discuss a variety of interactive learning spaces that you can incorporate into your library space, such as LEGO walls, whiteboard walls, and whiteboard tables. Seek out a variety of spaces and activities that encourage your students to be creative, even if it's just doodling for a few minutes while waiting for a friend to check out a book.

Participatory Learning as a Process

We care about our process as educators and sharers too. It's not just about getting curriculum. Content outcomes do not drive participatory learning; instead, makers drive the learning, which makes the learning much more individualized. We don't want to control what

people come away with—instead we want to design for the attitudes that they can come away with. We want to provide opportunities for learners to engage with content, gain confidence, have agency, and come away with new things to explore. We want them to leave the tinkering activity wanting to do more tinkering.

—Ryan Jenkins, Tinkering Studio Education Developer

The Tinkering Studio, a research and development lab open to the public inside of the Exploratorium, started off as a professional development studio that held workshops to help educators and developers "engage in the process of being a learner." Over the past five to six years, the space has morphed into an open lab on the floor of the museum that invites everyday patrons to participate in the research and development of ideas.

Ryan Jenkins, Tinkering Studio Education Developer, explains that the studio hosts many tinkering programs (including a free massive open online course [MOOC]) that entice educators to be "involved in tinkering" and help educators

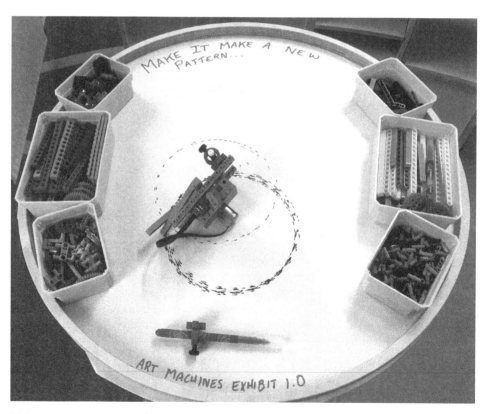

FIGURE 1.1   LEGO tinkering table (Picture by Amos Blanton). Version 1.0 of the Art Machines activity table. Art Machines is an activity developed by the Tinkering Studio at the Exploratorium and the LEGO Idea Studio at the LEGO Foundation. https://twitter .com/Lightnin99/status/768083105248870400.

"experiment with their own facilitation style." He suggests that educators should work toward getting learners involved early in the process and that educators do not have to be 100 percent sure of the outcome:

> We haven't figured everything out before we put activities out for museumgoers. Instead, we want learners to express their own ideas, get involved in their own process, and get excited about their own thoughts and ideas. This can be easier to facilitate when we put half- baked prototypes on the Tinkering floor.

Jenkins also stresses that educators should not hide their own learning process. Instead, he reiterates that we as educators should learn alongside our students and "engage learners in research and development of ideas." The "Tinker Educators" that facilitate these experiences at the Exploratorium try the activities themselves and reflect on what they find interesting and fascinating while exploring a new process or a new activity. Then when they engage students or museum patrons in a new activity, they share their own personal fascinations as a springboard for learning.

We are always tinkering with tinkering and process.
—Ryan Jenkins, Tinkering Studio Education Developer

Designing Half-Baked Prototypes That Entice Participation

It is important to get students involved early on in the process. When designing "half-baked prototypes" this still holds true. For the Tinkering Studio, they see the importance of students developing ideas, making mistakes, and problem-solving on their own to get beyond those mistakes. If you want to try activities out before sharing them with students, Jenkins suggests "making time to try something out as a learner, then reflect on that process. Put yourself in the learner's shoes, build a network of learners, and talk together about the experience as you work through the activity." When you are ready to try projects with students and crafting these types of experiences, make sure that your learners have an easy starting point and can experience success early on. If you notice that you have to spend 10 minutes explaining the project before anyone gets their hands on materials, you'll want to change something.

For a walk-up participatory experience, The Tinkering Studio focuses on providing a low threshold with wide walls that will lead to a variety of outcomes and a high ceiling (based on the *Design Principles for Tools that Support Creative Thinking* report by Resnick et al. 2005). Jenkins says that as they continue to develop half-baked prototypes, they attempt to make a wide variety of examples and then look for how participants interact with the sample projects. When thinking of activities, they ask themselves about participants: Do they try out different things? Is there a possibility to go further? Are people done quickly? If people only participate for a short amount of time, the Tinkering Studio educators realize that they have to change something—maybe materials, the prompt, or the facilitation.

Things to Consider When Crafting Participatory Activities—Tips from the Tinkering Studio

- Can participants have success early on? Can they still complexify over time?
- Can participants go deeper and learn more through continued exploration?
- Is there an element of playfulness?
- Is there a social element?
- Will it be inviting to a wide variety of people?
- Is it clear what tools, materials, and parts are being used?
- Can everyone have a unique outcome that reflects their own thinking?
- Is there a possibility to go deep into the learning process?

Make Time for Making

Time is a valuable asset in schools. Whether it's curriculum, standardized tests, state mandates, or otherwise, there is always something going on that demands the time of both teachers and students. This can make it difficult to pull students into the library for makerspace projects. If getting students into the makerspace during class time proves to be difficult, there are strategies for drawing students in at other times.

Host Maker Lunches

Students often don't get to visit the library for long enough to work on projects. One solution to this problem is to host maker lunches. This gets students into the makerspace at a time when they aren't constrained by classwork or teacher demands, and it can be a great way to bring in students who might not otherwise get to participate.

Consider themed and focused activities to start, such as LEGO challenge lunches, sewn circuit bracelets, and so on. These can help students get a better idea of what to expect and can help to form a more cohesive group, further developing the culture of creativity within your school. They're also excellent opportunities to build up your students' maker skills sets by turning the lunches into focused workshops, like those discussed in Chapter 4.

Inclusive Strategies

By hosting making activities during lunch, you will be able to accommodate students who would not be able to attend after school clubs due to transportation issues.

Free-Range Maker Time

While workshops and guided learning are important in an educational set-ting, it is still pertinent to offer free-range maker time throughout the school day. Allow students access to create in the library makerspace on their own terms. If you need to limit materials because of staffing issues, offer a badging system so that students can earn the right to access materials based on your setup. Then you can check out maker tools to students who have completed a series of tests or challenges. We go into further detail on this concept in Chapter 4. The important thing is that you give your students access to the materials in the library all throughout the school day.

Plus, we want students to feel like THEY can be anything or make any-thing they put their mind to. We want all of our students to feel like they can make something (or make meaning) at any point during the school day. *Creating a safe environment to be creative, to make mistakes, and to learn . . . has always been our school library motto.*

—Colleengraves.org

Free-range making is also important because our students are choosing to make something at school instead of passively sitting and zoning out on social media or a video game. Many times, making is highly engaging for students after they get over the hurdle of having to do something themselves with their own hands. Our students need a lot of practice with making things, which is why a balance of free-range time and guided instruction is essential. At our own schools, teachers are impressed when they see students who are normally "disengaged" and "unmotivated" in our library makerspace tinkering and mak-ing. We think the reason disengaged students like making is because it focuses on free choice. We don't tell them they have to build something a certain way or with certain materials during free-range making; instead, there is always student voice and choice involved.

Maker activities allow kids to not just freely create, but to pour their true heart and individual expression into something that won't be graded, judged, or otherwise rated in a way that might cause them to shut down. Allowing them to build in a failure-safe environment opens the door for students to engage in a way that makes their faces light up and experience things they might not have done on their own. Some important fact the student learned in the classroom that they weren't comprehending before might suddenly stick once they have the opportunity to put their understanding into something tangible and made by and with their own two hands.

—Stephen Tafoya, CHAOS Makerspace Manager
at Rapid City Public Library

Brand Your Space and Group

FIGURE 1.2 Stewart Makerspace banner.

Branding sometimes gets a bad rap, but it can actually go a long way in creating a consistent vocabulary and a better understanding among students and teachers. Consider ways to brand the space to make it clear what the purpose and goals of your space are.

When Diana Rendina first started her makerspace at Stewart Middle Magnet School, her teachers and students were confused about what to call it. She got passes from teachers for students to use the "library centers," to "play with LEGOs," to "make stuff," and so on. There wasn't a general understanding as to what exactly the space was and what purpose it served. She designed and printed a large vinyl sign with the words Stewart Makerspace on it and created custom library passes that included "makerspace" as one of the options for the student purpose in visiting the media center. Now her teachers and students are much more clear on what the space is and what students do there.

Consider designing a logo or hiring a graphic designer to make one (there might be a parent volunteer who's willing to do it for free in exchange for advertising in the school newsletter). Put that logo on all makerspace signage. Create T-shirts for student makers. Anytime you create anything related to the makerspace, use the logo and consistent wording and fonts. You will start to build a clear picture of what your makerspace is about and help your students and community feel a sense of identity in the space.

Action Steps

- Put together a Maker Steering Committee for your school.
- Write a mission and vision statement for your makerspace.
- Develop at least one creativity station in your library.
- Schedule your first maker lunch.
- Design a logo for your makerspace or have someone design it for you.

REFERENCES

Gershenfeld, Neil A. 2005. *Fab: The Coming Revolution on Your Desktop—from Personal Computers to Personal Fabrication.* New York: Basic Books.

Graves, Colleen. "Starting a School Makerspace from Scratch." Edutopia (blog). July 16, 2015. http://www.edutopia.org/blog/starting-school-makerspace-from-scratch-colleen-graves.

Jenkins, Ryan. "Collaborative R&D with Twitter, LEGO, and Digital Tools." *Sketchpad: Tinkering Studio* (blog). June 16, 2016. http://tinkering.exploratorium.edu/2016/05/17/twitter-lego-and-digital-tools.

The Makerspace Team. "The Makerspace Playbook: School Edition." *MakerEd.* February 2013. http://makered.org/wp-content/uploads/2014/09/Makerspace-Playbook-Feb-2013.pdf.

Resnick, M., and Eric Rosenbaum. 2013. "Designing for Tinkerability." In *Design, Make, Play: Growing the Next Generation of STEM Innovators*, edited by Margaret Honey and David Kanter, 163–181. New York: Routledge.

Resnick, M., B. Myers, K. Nakakoji, B. Shneiderman, R. Pausch, T. Selker, and M. Eisenberg. 2005. "Design Principles for Tools to Support Creative Thinking." Washington, D.C.: National Science Foundation workshop on Creativity Support Tools.

Simon, Nina. 2010. *The Participatory Museum.* Santa Cruz, CA: Museum 2.0.

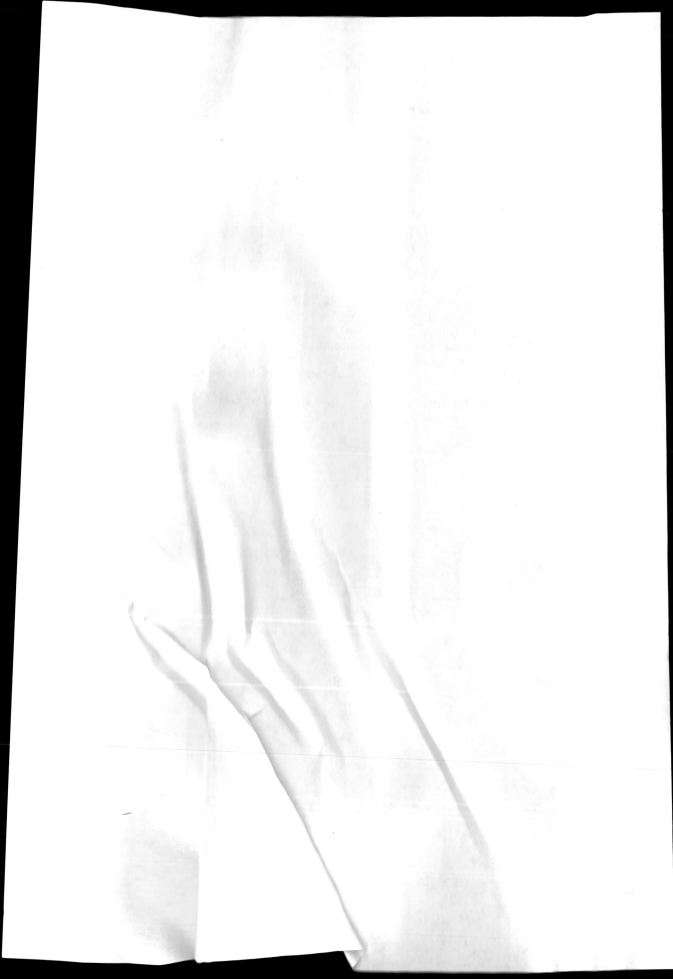

2

Expanding Learning to the Local and Global Maker Community

Creating a makerspace is about more than just connecting students with the school. Another critical aspect is connecting your students with both the local and global maker community. The Maker Movement is a massive, global movement, and it's important for students to understand their role. In addition, connecting your students with other makers gives them access to resources and knowledge that they wouldn't have otherwise.

CONNECTING LOCAL AND SCHOOL COMMUNITY THROUGH MAKER FESTS

Hosting a school-wide Maker Fest event can be a fantastic way to develop and grow a maker culture in your school. Based on the concept of Maker Faire©, a school-wide Maker Fest is kind of science fair meets hands-on learning in the most awesome way. It provides a venue for students to share their projects and become the teachers. One difference in our Maker Fest is that it focuses on student engagement and student organization. This student-driven Maker Faire gives you an opportunity to draw students, teachers, and classes into the makerspace who may have never visited it before and show them what it's all about. A Maker Fest is an excellent opportunity to develop some of those participatory maker stations discussed previously in Chapter 1. Maker Fest can be during school, after school, or a combination of both. Invite students, teachers, administrators, parents, community members, and district officials to share with and educate them about what is happening in the makerspace.

Students as Teachers

A core aspect of a school-wide Maker Fest is giving your students the opportunity to become teachers and leaders. Students are excited about teaching others how to make things. This can be through teaching members of the community about how certain makerspace technologies work or through guiding visitors in hands-on activities. It's beneficial to have a wide variety of activities and projects at a Maker Fest, as this can give you the opportunity to reach community members while they are on campus.

At Ann Richards School, Ana Josephson teaches a course called Maker Studio. This course is project-based learning at its finest, and during the first semester, she teaches the girls how to make lots of things. For the second semester, the girls are in charge of hosting, leading, and organizing a school-wide Maker Fest. In this student-led and student-driven festival, the girls come up with activities to make with attendees. Ana says that this experience leaves the students feeling empowered. "They grow and feel a sense of pride. Plus, it gives our kids something to talk about with adults that is significant and they are passionate about. It is a real experience for them to share, and it motivates them to do more."

In addition to having students teach skills and lead activities, provide opportunities for students to share projects that they have made throughout the school year. Usually these tend to be larger and more interactive projects. At the 2016 Stewart Maker Fest, students let guests explore a cardboard maker cave that they had built. Parents and other visitors could try their hand at a giant crossbow made out of K'nex and learn about the process students went through to build a K'nex roller coaster. One of the biggest hits of the Maker Fest was a giant cardboard obstacle course. Guests had to guide Sphero, a robotic ball, through the obstacle course, knock over a barricade holding up Dot, another robot, and then escape. All of this had to happen without getting tagged by Dash, a third robot, which was controlled by the student who designed the course.

One can take this concept even further as Laura Fleming's students did with MakerJam. This event was created by students for students and invited students to create anything based on a theme given only 24 hours before the event. Fleming described the intention behind MakerJam:

> The hope was that MakerJam would be an experience that inspired creativity in students of all kinds—from those that have never had the time, environment, or motivation to create, to those makers that have been waiting for a chance to showcase their creativity without having to conform to or fit the traditional art or talent show, to those that regularly create but have never been challenged by limits on time and planning. (2016)

Maker Fest as Community Engagement

A school-wide Maker Fest is an excellent opportunity to bring members of your community together and share the learning of your students. In addition to inviting parents, students, teachers, and administrators, consider inviting other makers within the community. Local makerspaces, local public libraries, crafters, artisans, and many other would love to come and share about what they do with your school. Many will likely be willing to teach a maker skill at their booth, providing another hands-on learning opportunity for guests and attendees.

Inviting community makers is also a great way to encourage parents and students to continuing making even when school is not in session. By connecting them with local makerspaces and public libraries, they can learn about other classes, workshops, and activities that can allow them to continue to explore making outside of school.

Bringing Classes and Students to Maker Fest

If you hold your Maker Fest during school hours, teachers can bring their classes to the event, providing an amazing opportunity to connect your greater student body with making. Depending on the school, a schedule might be set for students to visit during their science classes, or you might just work with individual teachers who are interested and supportive. By having classes come during school, you are able to reach those students who aren't able to come to after-school events, as well as those who might not be inclined on their own but might just discover that they're makers themselves.

A Maker Fest during school allows students to lurk and explore with no risk, especially those who might not always be inclined to join regular makerspace activities. At the 2016 Maker Fest at Stewart Middle Magnet School, students from the school's Stewart Makers Club shared with their fellow students throughout the day about circuits, robotics, and arts and crafts projects. Many students came back more than once to continue tinkering and checking the projects that their peers had made.

Inviting Experts through Skype

At Ryan High School, Colleen invited Makey Makey co-inventor Jay Silver to examine student projects during their Invention Literacy Maker Fest. Through the awesome power of videoconferencing, Jay was able to "sit down" and chat with each group of makers. The students were able to hold casual conversations about their process of invention and the challenges they faced through each iteration of a prototype. Students loved having Jay Silver visit via Skype, and even though they were nervous at first, they warmed to how casually Jay chatted with them to learn about their work. Just as you would for any other videoconference or in-person visit, it is crucial to prepare students ahead of time. Colleen prepped students by having them discuss ideas centered around invention literacy, the historical context of their invention, and told them to be ready to discuss the most challenging part of creating each invention.

During Colleen's Girls in Tech Camp, the students Skyped with Jie Qi, inventor of Chibitronics, to learn more about how paper circuits work and get tips when crafting with copper tape and circuitry. The students loved getting real advice from an expert. Plus, it helped enhance their worldview of making. (You can read more about this camp in Chapter 4.)

CONNECTING MAKERS THROUGH DIGITAL MEDIA

Whenever possible, create a way for your makers to connect with one another, interact with others, and share their creations outside of school. We are naturally social creatures, but, unfortunately, social time is often sparse at school. By creating an online community centered around your makerspace, you can give students opportunities to share and connect in a safe space. What shape this takes will vary depending on grade level and social media policies within your district. Luckily, myriad options for connecting and sharing digitally can work beautifully within a makerspace.

Connecting with Maker Discussions

If your school or district uses a classroom management system (CMS), such as Edmodo or Edsby, create a group for your makers within its framework. Start discussions about what projects students are working on, and encourage them to share pictures of their work. Harness that group of students you identified in your student advisory committee as moderators—often the best conversations come when started by fellow students. If the system allows for polls, use it to survey your students about what their favorite materials and projects are, what their favorite areas of the library makerspace are, and so on. This can provide invaluable insight as your library makerspace continues to grow and evolve.

Connecting through Social Media

Create a professional social media account as a librarian and one for your makerspace. Make sure to follow the top leaders in the field and others who are starting or running makerspaces to ensure a constant feed of successful projects, fresh ideas, and working examples. Be sure to contribute your own content such as photos, videos, and lesson ideas so that you can glean feedback from your maker community.

Because projects in makerspaces tend to be primarily visual, social media networks that allow photo and video sharing are ideal. It's also good to have networks where you can share links to digital projects, such as student coding projects or digital audio recordings. Look into networks that allow you to upload and display media, such as Flickr (for photos) and SoundCloud (for audio). This can be a great way to create an archive of the projects your students are making.

One unique way you can share iterations of prototypes and even track the process of student makes is to build your own Spin turntable (directions available at http://spin.media.mit.edu). Tiffany Tseng of MIT Media Lab created this "photography turntable system that lets you capture how your DIY projects come together over time." The Spin turntable allows you to capture the build process and different iterations of a project with a GIF or a video that students can then easily share over social media. Colleen's students tinkered with this process during their Invention Literacy Project. Now, Colleen is instituting a Spin turntable that will always be available so that all makers can keep track of their progress with this amazing Arduino-based invention.

If district social media policies allow, consider creating a Facebook page for your makerspace. This can be an excellent way to connect with parents, students, and community members. Facebook is a great way to announce programs, workshops, and other events. You can create photo albums of the projects that students have created. A Facebook group can also be a great way to share links and resources that can help parents and students continue embracing making and creativity at home.

Consider creating a common hashtag for all posts related to your makerspace and for special maker events. Because librarians love data and organization, hashtags are also helpful in tracking events, projects, special classes, and more. Invite your students to follow the hashtag and to use it in their own social media posts. At Stewart Middle Magnet School, Diana Rendina used the hashtag #stewartmakes anytime she posts something related to projects her students are making. Colleen used #inventionliteracy and #rhsmakes throughout their special maker-focused research. By utilizing social media in the library makerspace, you bring the conversation about making and creativity straight to your students' phones and computers, which is the best place to get (and keep) their attention. Plus, students get really excited when they see their work on the Internet and often want to show it to their friends, thus continuing to build the maker culture within your school. Lastly, with Twitter's easy-to-use search engine, you can quickly feature and recall favorite projects by searching your hashtag.

Connecting through Blogging and Other Platforms

Creating a blog specifically for your library makerspace can be a powerful way to share what students are working on and engage them in the discussion. Look into blogging platforms that allow students to add posts and consider inviting a different student to post each week. Blogs are powerful tools in that they can allow you to share just about any type of media, link, and text. Bear in mind, however, that they can be time-consuming. Try to delegate the writing rather than doing it all yourself—it will give your students a sense of ownership and will make them more likely to actually read and visit the blog. Read through Chapter 8 to see how one teacher used blogging to track an annual engineering project.

There are other platforms where students can share projects as well. Instructables.com allows members to create tutorials on how to do just about anything. Create an Instructables account for your makerspace, or encourage students to create their own (they must be at least 13 years old and have parent permission) and to write and post tutorials about their projects (Autodesk

2013). Even if students are not old enough yet to create their own accounts, they can still use Instructables to get great ideas for projects.

Some vendor sites have sharing and user communities built in to their web pages. littleBits has a fantastic online community where members can share projects that they've created using the tiny magnetic circuits. SparkFun has instituted a great web space for educators and student inventors called Inventor Space where educators can create classes and students can share inventions (https://invent.sparkfun.com).

CONNECTING YOUR STUDENTS WITH THOSE OUTSIDE OF THE LIBRARY

The majority of our students have had limited life experiences and rarely see life outside of their city. While some students might have families that travel frequently, many may have never traveled outside of the state. Yet, our world today is more connected than ever through the power of technology and social media. The Maker Movement is a huge, global movement, and it's important to help your students gain a sense that they are a part of something greater. Depending on your district, your students may or may not have a library makerspace at the next stop on their educational journey. By introducing them to makers beyond school, students can make connections, garner a worldview, and gain creative confidence.

Connecting with Your Local Maker Community

Part of the power of the Maker Movement is connecting with your local maker community. Most likely, there are other makers in your area who will welcome you and your students with open arms. Makers love to share and give and are happy to teach others about what they do. Finding your local maker community and connecting your students with them will increase your maker connections and help to ensure makerspace success.

Visit Local Makerspaces

The first and easiest place to start in connecting with your local maker community is to visit local makerspaces. More and more makerspaces are popping up all over. Some are nonprofits. Some are in public libraries. Visit these places. Take classes on a new technique. Share about what you're doing at your school (or what you're hoping to start doing). Take pictures, share on social media, and make connections with makers at these spaces.

After you've built your own personal connection with your local makerspaces, get your students connected with them as well. Share information about classes at the space with your students. If possible, organize a field trip to the space—makerspaces are often havens for innovators and entrepreneurs, and visiting these types of spaces can easily tie in with curriculum.

Connect with local makerspaces early on, as you can both benefit. Larger makerspaces might have access to tools and funding that you aren't able to have in your makerspace. You have regular access to students who might become regulars at the community makerspace. It's a win-win situation. Colleen was able to share resources with the Denton Public Library to teach her students how to solder. (Read more in Chapter 4.)

Local Maker Events

Another excellent way to find and connect with makers in your community is to attend local maker events. Find out where the nearest Maker Faire is and make plans to attend. Bring a group of students with you and have them help you brainstorm what experiences you could bring back to your school. Build your maker network by introducing yourself and connecting with makers at Maker Faire. People at these events love to share. David Lang (2013) experienced this firsthand when he decided to go from "Zero to Maker." He attended a local Maker Faire, began visiting spaces, and was determined to become an "engaged active participant" of life! Lang found that, "I had to choose to become a beginner, to get comfortable with mistakes, to ask a lot of questions, and to seek out the right teachers. After I crossed that bridge, everything else fell into place. Makers are a community of beginners, and we're all learning together" (2013, 12).

Maker Faires aren't the only type of maker event. Look for events happening in your public library. Consider robotics competitions, craft fairs, and coding clubs. The more you look, the more makers you will find. Visit local community markets, find tool-lending libraries, and be vigilant for maker-focused events where you can learn, share, and grow.

Invite Makers into Your Library

While field trips to local makerspaces and maker events are awesome, you will be limited in the number of students that you are able to reach this way. Because of this, it is imperative that you invite makers into your library to share. Makers can be amazing guest speakers and often bring along projects to share and activities to teach students. Think beyond traditional makers in this as well. Laura Fleming (2015) invited a bicycle mechanic to speak to her students in her makerspace. He taught students about the basics of bicycle maintenance.

Before Colleen had any funding for her makerspace at Lamar, she held a coding bonanza and helped the students work through lessons on Code.org, begin the basics of learning Scratch programming, and tinker with Arduino code. She wanted to take things further and let the students meet and interact with a real game developer. Luckily, one of her art school friends had not only made and created games but was more than willing to chat with the kids about the realities of his profession. Students learned that it takes a team of game developers months to create simple web games. Others were inspired to share their own game ideas with this expert and overjoyed when he said they had great and unique game ideas.

When looking for makers to invite into your library, don't forget to look to parents and the school community as well. You may have parents or siblings of students at your school who are engineers, mechanics, graphic designers, artists, and more. Colleen had a student aide at Lamar whose brother built amazing structures in Minecraft and was glad to share his expertise with students after school. You don't have to wait for the Great American Teach-In to invite these parents and family members to speak at your school. Having parents come and share about their work and their experiences will help build your maker community and strengthen your students' connection to the Maker Movement.

Connecting on a Global Level

In addition to connecting your students to the Maker Movement at a local level, look for ways to connect them at a global level as well. This movement is huge, and there are numerous opportunities to connect your students with other kids from around the world. Great power comes from linking your students to other makers far and wide. It helps them to develop a sense of connectedness and expands their horizons.

Video Conferencing

One of the easiest ways to connect your students to makers around the world is through videoconferencing. Thanks to amazing tools such as Skype, Google Hangouts, Zoom, Nepris, and Voxer, it's easier than ever to talk to someone in real time no matter where they're located. Videoconferences can be used to connect your students with makers and experts related to projects that they're working on. You can also connect with other schools to share projects (more on this in the next section). Even a videoconference with another school from your district can connect your students with others that they might never meet otherwise. It's actually how Colleen and Diana met!

It's best to try to prepare the students for the videoconference ahead of time. Share with them about who you'll be talking to and why. If the expert has a website or YouTube channel, explore these resources together. On the day of the videoconference, be prepared to take control of things if you need to. Have students prepare questions ahead of time and plan for how you will call them up and encourage interactivity. But don't be afraid to go with the flow and see how things happen. Often some of the best conversations and interactions happen quite serendipitously. Colleen had her #Girlsintech camp interview a designer from littleBits, Krystal Persaud, to help her students see some of the ways that women are involved in tech careers. The lively conversation turned into a deep learning experience about industrial design and user-centered design!

One powerful aspect of videoconferences is that they can enable student voices among those who are often reluctant to share. During a videoconference with a local elementary school, Diana Rendina's students were sharing some K'nex projects they had recently created. One of the students in this group was a bit shy and socially awkward. Although he didn't get along well with others and tended to keep to himself, he was one of the first students to volunteer to go up to the microphone and share his project. As the second graders he was sharing with were "oohing" and "ahhing" over his project, you could see his confidence soar. This was a student who would *never* have volunteered first to present in front of the class. The power of sharing with others through videoconferencing gave him a voice.

Inclusive Strategies

Videoconferencing can be a powerful way to give a voice to students who might not always speak up in the classroom. When preparing for a videoconference, be intentional about including those students who tend not to speak up. If needed, prep students with questions before the conference.

In addition, use videoconferences to connect students with female and minority makers and tech leaders as they can become powerful role models.

You'll be surprised at how many students might act like they do not want to participate until the videoconference starts. Students new to Skyping with experts may be nervous and shy at first, but by the end of the conversation, your students will be fighting over the microphone!

During a chat with the Tinkering Studio, Colleen watched some of her students go from reluctant participants to active, engaged learners. Many were nervous to chat with these experts from the Exploratorium, but after they saw how relaxed and interactive educator Ryan Jenkins and director Karen Wilkinson were, they were jumping up to ask questions about tinkering and inventing.

Joint Design Challenges with Other Schools

Simply talking with students from another school and sharing ideas and projects can be powerful. But to develop a deeper sense of global connectedness for your students, consider collaborating with another school to host a joint design challenge with your students. Consider using some of the suggestions in Chapters 4, 6, and 7, or come up with your own ideas. Ideally, you'll want to have both schools first learn about the challenge in a videoconference together. After it's set, continue to share your projects with each other through social media. At the end of the design challenge, meet up again so students can share their projects with one another. This meeting sometimes becomes a fun, hectic show-and-tell, but it can be powerful for students, and they will reminisce on the experience for weeks.

One of the first ways Diana Rendina's and Colleen Graves's students connected was through a joint design challenge. At the initial videoconference, Colleen's students shared how to make brushbots, and Diana's students shared their Caine's Arcade Cardboard Challenge projects. After the sharing was done, the students at Lamar Middle School suggested a Catapult Challenge to the students of Stewart Middle Magnet. This initial show and tell helped our students get to know one another and feel comfortable challenging makers to a friendly maker challenge. Each school began working on a variety of projects centered around this theme of "catapults." Gradually, the project expanded to become the "make something that flings something without poking out your friend's eye" challenge as students designed trebuchets, crossbows, ballistas, and a variety of other devices. Diana and Colleen shared the projects their students were creating via Twitter. At the end of the challenge, both schools met up again. The energy in the rooms was high as students at Lamar showed off their giant wooden water bottle launcher as tall as the students, while students at Stewart were thrilled that their LEGO trebuchet held together for the launch. These types of events can be nerve-wracking for adults. Colleen remembered being nervous that no one would show up with a working catapult. However, the morning of the scheduled Skype, two boys rolled in a catapult on a garden cart from Home Depot. On the side of their catapult, the boys had written with marker, "My catapult will launch your catapult." Another student brought in a five-armed catapult. So as nervous as you may be to set out a challenge and host a Skype with another school, remember that your students will rise to the occasion and let their genius shine in their creations.

Social Media Tinkering Instigations

Another way to invite global participation centered around making is to follow social media trends and be open to sharing and learning from other museums and libraries. At the end of the 2016 school year, Colleen noticed some other Texas libraries and maker educator Josh Burker creating interesting tinkering explorations based on #LEGOtinkering. The fine folks at the Tinkering Studio like Lianna Kali started experimenting with linkages during Noga Elhassid's artist in residence. Jenkins and Wilkinson from the Tinkering Studio quickly found that through social media, libraries and museums could take "initial ideas around art machines, sound makers, and linkages to new and unexpected places" (Jenkins 2016). Colleen latched onto some strange LEGO linkage inventions from the Tinkering Studio and shared them with students as a springboard for the Invention Literacy project. She also shared some novice LEGO makers with them and watched as the students used these ideas of linkages and attempted to incorporate littleBits into their LEGO tinkering. In a blog post, Jenkins discussed the ideas behind creating a social media tinkering instigation: "I think there's [a] trick to creating shared problem spaces that are open ended enough to allow for personal expression but focused enough that ideas are related and can spread quickly" (2016). (Read more about the Tinkering Studio Design Prompts in Chapter 5.)

Inclusive Strategies

Social media can also be a powerful voice for students who normally experience loss of voice in the classroom. Some students who would not share in front of their peers will shine via social networks.

Social media can also be a great way to connect with female and minority makers.

Global Maker Service Projects

Even though it may not seem like it from how popular culture portrays them, students care deeply about helping others. They like knowing that the things they create can help other people and make the world a better place. Global maker service projects are a great way to help your students use design thinking and creativity to help others. It could be as simple as a sewing workshop to create dog beds for a local animal shelter. Look for local charities and organizations that you can partner with. These make for excellent service learning opportunities because your students can visit these locations and see the impact of their work firsthand.

In addition to local service projects, there are powerful opportunities to engage your students in global maker service learning projects. There are many opportunities like this, including Students Rebuild and Global Youth Service Day. If there isn't an opportunity, you can create one! In 2014, Shannon Miller and her school, Van Meter, partnered with In This Together Media to create the Banding Together project (Miller, 2014). This was at the height of the Rainbow Loom band craze. Shannon's students had been working on research projects around Rainbow Loom bands when they were contacted about the possibility of making bracelets for children in India. They videoconferenced with some teachers in India and learned more about the communities they lived in. The students started creating bracelets and writing notes to the children they were sending them too. Soon, other schools joined in on the project, and it evolved into a global movement. This was an amazing opportunity for students in a small, rural community to connect with others all around the world.

Gina Seymour[1] runs a MakerCare program at Islip High School dedicated to nurturing philanthropic qualities while benefiting organizations both local and global. Collaborating with service-based clubs in her school and cultivating partnerships with outside agencies, students carry out hands-on service projects and take an active role in making a difference in their community and the world.

From creating sleeping mats for the homeless using plastic yarn made from grocery bags to using recycled fabric from T-shirts and jeans to make dog toys for animal shelters, students convert discarded materials into something useful. Donated pillowcases are used to make dresses for African schoolgirls,

---

1. Information regarding and quotes from Gina Seymour are from a telephone interview by the author on July 7, 2016.

which are then donated to Little Dresses for Africa. There is an emphasis on environmental sustainability in addition to helping others. Students help protect our world by repurposing discarded items to reduce the human impact on the environment and curtail excess garbage in our landfills. Students learn they can make a positive environmental and philanthropic impact on their world.

Impact of Connected Learning on Students

Throughout this chapter, we've offered you advice and stories on transforming a school library into a participatory learning space, growing a maker community within your school, and using in-person interactions and modern technology to connect students with the world. But even with all this, it is still possible for some to be skeptical as to how these types of experiences benefit students.

Connectedness and the Four Cs

Thanks to modern technology and social media, we live in an increasingly disconnected world. We stare at our screens all day and have swapped out our in-person social interactions for digital ones. And while there are certainly many amazing benefits to social media, if that's the only way we ever connect with others, we start to feel disconnected from our communities and those around us.

A large part of participatory learning is creating social learning experiences. At a time when students are learning the dynamics of socialization, participatory learning can play a vital role in their development.

Consider this story of two hypothetical students. In a makerspace, a student is physically working on a project with his hands, often at the same table as other students. He starts to talk and share about his projects. He takes an interest in what another student is doing, and suddenly they're a team. They start to run into some problems with how the project is coming together, so the two students agree to meet up again at lunch the next day to continue working on it. They're so pleased with how the project turned out, that they ask to showcase it at the school Maker Faire. At the event, both students are speaking with total strangers and sharing with them about how their project came together. They create a video together about their project and share it on YouTube, where they receive comments and questions from all around the world.

This narrative is not an uncommon experience in participatory learning spaces. You'll notice that the students experienced creativity (building the project), collaboration (working on it together), critical thinking (solving when things didn't go as planned), and communication (sharing about it with others). These Four Cs (creativity, collaboration, critical thinking, and communication) are considered essential skills for students in the 21st century.

Furthers Student Impact and Voice

When a student creates a project knowing that only her teacher and maybe one of two other classmates will ever see it, the incentive to make the project amazing is low. But if she knows that dozens of people will see her project at a Maker Fest, through a videoconference, or on social media, suddenly her project gains significantly more importance. Now she isn't just designing her project for her teacher—she's designing it for the world and an authentic audience.

By giving our students connected learning experiences within their community and the world, we amplify their voices. Student voice is neglected in so many schools. Students are left feeling that they are unable to have an impact on their world or to make a difference. Provide students with participatory and connected learning experiences, and they will begin to realize the power that their voices have.

Transforms Students into Creators Rather Than Consumers

We live in a consumption-driven culture. With the click of a few buttons, an item can be ordered and delivered without ever leaving the comfort of your home. There is a product out there for just about every need, whether or not we knew that we needed it. Many of these products are designed to quickly wear out and trap us into a pattern of consumption.

Because there is so much power in establishing a culture of creativity while developing participatory learning experiences, there is an extreme value in connected learning experiences for our students. When we offer our students these experiences, we are teaching them to be creators rather than consumers. We are empowering them to come up with their own ideas and solutions, to think critically about the world, and become active participants. And through this, we are preparing them to be responsible citizens of the world.

Action Steps

- Start planning a Maker Fest for your school.
- Find an expert to Skype with your students.
- Create at least one social media account to share your makerspace activities.
- Visit a local makerspace and make connections.
- Find another school to plan a joint design challenge.

REFERENCES

Fleming, Laura. "MakerJam Energizes K–12 Education with Themed Hackathons." *Make.* June 21, 2016. http://makezine.com/2016/06/21/makerjam-make -something-anything.

Fleming, Laura. 2015. *Worlds of Making: Best Practices for Establishing a Maker-space for Your School.* Newbury Park, CA: Corwin.

Jenkins, Ryan. "Collaborative R&D with Twitter, LEGO, and Digital Tools." *Sketchpad: Tinkering Studio* (blog). June 22, 2016. http://tinkering.exploratorium .edu/2016/05/17/twitter-lego-and-digital-tools.

Lang, David. 2013. *Zero to Maker: Learn (Just Enough) to Make (Just About) Anything.* San Francisco: Maker Media.

"Legal Notices & Trademarks." *Autodesk.* June 5, 2013. http://www.autodesk.com /company/legal-notices-trademarks/terms-of-service-autodesk360-web-services /instructables-terms-of-service-june-5-2013.

Miller, Shannon M. "'Banding Together' Project." *Smore.* 2014. https://www.smore .com/n65m-students-schools-banding-together.

3

Crafting Interactive Spaces

When creating challenged-based learning activities for students, the design of the learning space may seem like an afterthought. However, spending some time planning, designing, and crafting a dynamic, interactive environment for students can go a long way in sparking creativity. Learning space design theory is a fascinating and constantly evolving field. Applying strategies based on these theories can transform your library.

The traditional school library environment was not designed with today's students nor today's uses in mind. Heavy wooden tables, furniture bolted to the floor, wall-to-wall bookshelves, minimal outlets, and domineering circulation desks are all common sights in many school libraries. Even those built in recent years are often designed primarily with the purposes of book storage and quiet reading spaces in mind. While it is still possible to have participatory learning and maker activities in such an environment, one quickly finds this outdated model to be a hindrance to learning. With some creativity and a bit of elbow grease, it's possible to transform your space, even with little to no funding for renovation.

Stewart Middle Magnet School was built in 1955 as a segregated high school. The building was renovated in the 1970s into a seventh grade center, and, at that point, the cafeteria was converted into the media center. Offices and storage rooms were created, and the windows were bricked over because that was the trend at the time. Since then, the physical space and the collection have gone through many changes, as the school switched from being a seventh grade center to a magnet middle school. The layout before Diana Rendina got there had been very traditional—shelves along every inch of available wall space, floor stacks taking up tons of room, and a computer lab in rows. There was only one area with comfortable chairs for reading at the time. Diana gradually culled down the collection, got rid of unnecessary shelving, and opened up space for students to relax, study, and create.

Colleen moved into a very traditional library in 2015 where students walked into oversized chairs, old printers, and tons of reference books. Knowing that

FIGURE 3.1 DHS café seating.

students still enjoyed traditional activities in this space, she had to be mindful when redesigning. She also knew the furniture was fairly new, so readjusting the space would have to do in the initial redesign. Plus, many empty bookshelves could be moved to create different types of learning spots around the library.

Other things to consider are the size, general shape, and consistency of your library. Aaron Graves's library at Denton High School had gone through so many renovations and shape shifts that it no longer held uniformity as a space. Aaron enlisted the art club and some other individuals to design murals. The school loves its tradition and heritage, and he wanted the murals to reflect the city and school spirit. One mural features landmarks from the city, the local university, and the school while the other captures the slogans, motto, and spirit of the school. To take advantage of the focal points created by the murals, Aaron removed all the catalog computers along this wall and set up 3D printers in this area. Now these 3D printers are the first thing students see when they come in, and the space continues to draw them in as they see other students tinkering at worktables (see Figure 3.1). It gives students a chance to immediately see what activities are going on that day, whether it's holding a workshop or just tinkering. They can participate in making or move on to a quiet area and read if needed. The focal areas give the space structure and flow, which is something the previous renovations took away.

LEARNING SPACE DESIGN THEORY

There is a sizable body of research on how learning spaces affect student achievement and well-being. Some works focus specifically on school library spaces, while others focus on learning spaces in general. But whether or not the work is focused specifically on school libraries, all educators can still learn a great deal from them. Many of the design principles that work well in classroom and common spaces can also have direct applications to the learning environments created within school libraries.

Types of Active Learning Spaces

Traditionally, the library was seen as a passive learning environment. Students come in, select a book or other research material, and read quietly. With the advent of computers, this model continued, only now students were consuming their reference materials digitally, often in computer labs that hinder collaboration. A shift from this style of learning to a more active, collaborative learning environment is happening. Libraries no longer have to be perfectly quiet, pristine environments. Students are coming in to collaborate on group projects, to give presentations to their classes, and to create digital works on computers. They're coming to build, tinker, or find a safe place to read a book. Libraries have to support whole class instruction, small groups, and individual learning styles. In order for the library to support all these uses, a variety of active learning spaces are needed. Basye et al. (2015) identify six examples of learning spaces that support digital age learning: small-group areas, large-group areas; technology-rich areas; quiet, solitary areas; community accessible areas; and makerspaces. Although their research focused on learning environments as a whole rather than specifically on school libraries, intentionally designing library spaces to include these types of environments can ensure that all students' needs are being met, no matter what their learning style.

Small-Group Areas

Small-group areas provide a space for students to collaborate in groups for discussion and brainstorming, as well as planning and creating projects (Basye et al. 2015). Ideally, this area would be somewhat separated from other parts of the library, allowing students a sense of privacy. Partial screens, diner-style booths, glassed-in rooms, or shelving can all be used to help create that sense of privacy. How these types of spaces play out will vary from one school to the next. Schools that are 1:1 or bring your own device (BYOD) might find that a teaming table with a monitor is ideal for a small-group area because students can share and collaborate on their own digital devices. Whiteboard tables that can support multiple students can be excellent for small-group brainstorming. Small-group areas with comfortable, soft furnishings can support discussion, debate, and reflection.

At Ryan High School, Colleen moved old periodicals from the wall-to-wall shelves that domineered the front of the library. Instead of keeping the quiet reading zone at the front of the library with the most foot traffic, she moved the comfortable oversized chairs to the back of the library and brought in a few round tables and chairs for students to be able to work in small-groups and have lunch in this area. Instead of periodicals, Colleen created a showcase of the best and newest books sorted by genre (see Figure 3.2).

FIGURE 3.2 Showcase/lunch/small-group area at Ryan High School.

Diana got rid of the heavy wooden library tables at Stewart Middle Magnet School and replaced them with lightweight tables on casters. Students can now easily use this area to work on projects in small groups, and they can quickly reconfigure the arrangement to suit their needs.

Large-Group Areas

Most school libraries already have a large-group area in the form of class instruction space. This space is ideal for whole-class instruction and student presentations. Often, this space also ends up fulfilling the purpose of the community area as well, but this will vary from school to school. Because challenge-based learning doesn't focus on a lecture format, focus on flexible furnishings so the large-group area can support more active styles of learning and collaboration. However, there should be a space where the entire group can gather together for instructions and host student presentations. Tables on casters that can flip and nest, chairs that are lightweight and ergonomic, and whiteboard-covered surfaces are all ideal for a large-group area. A permanent digital presentation should also be set up in this area with a screen, projector, and dedicated computer.

Some libraries have large classroom areas separated but still inside the library, and some are more open concept. At Ryan High School, Colleen has two large classroom areas on opposite sides of the library. These spaces are great for learning, but sound can travel if both classroom areas are in use. Luckily, lowering the projector screen works as a great sound barrier. If both classrooms aren't in use, students are welcome to use these spaces for small-group collaborations. Use what you already have to its fullest potential when

FIGURE 3.3   Class instruction area at Stewart Middle Magnet School.

crafting interactive spaces, and remember to listen to students' ideas when redesigning. They often have the best ideas.

At Stewart Middle Magnet School, Diana Rendina created a class instruction space by removing some wall shelves, mounting a whiteboard and projector to the wall, and changing out the traditional library furniture for flexible tables and chairs (see Figure 3.3).

Technology-Rich Areas

Most modern school libraries already have a computer lab or at least some student computer access. With a focus on challenged-based learning, however, a traditional computer lab is not always compatible. Rows of computers all facing the same direction (or worse, facing a wall) are geared toward students facing the front of the "room" and awaiting instruction. Aim for creating smaller, collaborative clusters that can still be used by a whole class. In addition, consider other types of technology your library can support. Having tablets or Chromebooks available for students to check out can provide excellent opportunities for supporting a variety of learning styles. Especially if your school is 1:1 or BYOD, consider investing in a few high-powered desktop computers to function as creative media centers loaded with software for photo editing, video editing, audio recording, and graphic design. This will help to support students with programs and resources that they may not have access to at home.

It's important to take into consideration the technology used by district campuses and students before making major technology purchases. Because Ryan

High School functions primarily on Chromebooks, buying tablets is unproductive. When Colleen was at a 1:1 district, she used her iPad on a daily basis, but once her students didn't have iPads, she noticed her own personal iPad usage dropping off. Educators tend to use the technology that their students use the most. Therefore, let the familiarity, purpose, and usefulness drive your technology purchases instead of jumping on technology bandwagons.

Quiet and Solitary Spaces

Traditionally, school libraries have been quiet, solitary reading rooms. Modern school libraries, by contrast, are often buzzing with activity. Even with all of the activity and noise in a modern library, librarians still need to recognize and honor the needs of students who need a quiet, solitary space to focus. If space is large enough to support it, create quiet zones or even a quiet room, where it is understood that conversation is limited so that focused studying and reading can occur. If only one giant room is available, look for ways to rearrange the furniture to create smaller, private nooks. Soft furnishings can also help to dampen and absorb noise.

Move quiet reading spots to the lowest foot traffic area in the library, that is, away from the circulation desk and front door. Colleen weeded out her non-fiction collection and removed some extra library shelves in the back of her library to create space for readers. By doing this, she was able to move her comfy seating right next to big beautiful windows in a well-lighted archway (see Figure 3.4), which also helped eliminate noise as voices tend to carry in this spot. It's important to realize that you may need to de-program the area when you make changes like this. You'll have to teach your students about how to behave in the quiet areas, and remind them often where collaborative work is encouraged.

FIGURE 3.4A Ryan High School reading area (before).

FIGURE 3.4B Ryan High School reading area (after).

Stewart Middle Magnet School is one large, open room, so creating a quiet zone was a challenge. Diana was able to accomplish this by shifting some existing floor shelving units to create small reading nooks large enough for one or two people (see Figure 3.5). While these spaces aren't perfectly quiet, they still help to eliminate distractions so that students can focus.

FIGURE 3.5 Stewart Middle Magnet School reading nook.

Makerspaces

Because the focus of this book is on supporting challenge-based learning in the school library makerspace, hopefully your library already has a space where students can tinker, create, and build. Remember that makerspaces come in all shapes and sizes, and a huge budget or a ton of space is not needed to create one within a library. Try to find a way to give students access to hands-on materials where they can explore new ideas and have creative play experiences. For the purposes of challenge-based learning, it is ideal to have a mix of non-consumable, reusable materials (e.g., LEGOs and K'nex), and consumable materials (e.g., arts and crafts supplies, cardboard and everyday recyclables). In addition, look to include prototyping tools and supplies that can be used with a variety of projects, such as tape, rubber bands, hot glue guns, rulers, scissors, and so on.

One of the most important aspects of your makerspace will be organizing storage. Many makerspace materials and tools can be quite expensive, so the natural inclination may be to keep them as secure as possible to avoid theft or damage. However, it's important to balance this with visibility—if a supply can't be seen, it's less likely to be used (Doorley and Witthoft 2010). Aim to keep things as accessible as possible, and only lock up supplies when absolutely needed, such as over long weekends or holiday breaks. Colleen experimented with a variety of storage options such as tool bin organizers and checking out expensive materials, and she has now settled on clear, labeled storage containers. To make these items accessible, they are placed in a highly visible

FIGURE 3.6A   Ryan High School clearly labeled makerspace storage.

space in her library. Almost all of her makerspace materials and tools are located on shelves to the left of the circulation desk. These clearly labeled makerspace tools are at the forefront of the library and also in constant view by library staff, thus keeping them secure and accessible (see Figures 3.6A and B). Students are free to use most materials, but some materials require workshop experience or badging before students are able to use them freely. Badging and skill workshops are explored further in the next chapter.

Tools of an Active Learning Space

Within any type of active learning space, several types of tools and furnishings can help to support student learning. Many of these may already be present in the library; some may have to be sourced creatively or funding sought for, but it is worth taking the time to try to include these in your library space. Having these types of tools and furnishings will help to support the development of the Four Cs—creativity, collaboration, critical thinking, and communication skills—in students.

Flexible Furnishings

The more flexible space can be, the better. Modular, flexible furnishings allow students and teachers to take ownership of the space, reconfiguring it as needed

FIGURE 3.6B Close-up view of Ryan High School clearly labeled makerspace storage.

for their purposes. Locking casters on tables are fantastic for this, as they allow for easy, quick transitions and for stability after the desired layout is in place. Flip and nest tables are also a fantastic option because they can be easily moved out of the way, creating larger, open spaces (great for many maker activities). Try to also include a variety of table sizes, heights, and shapes to allow for an even greater number of configurations and to support students in both large and small groups.

Writable Surfaces

Writable surfaces are fantastic for student brainstorming, designing prototypes, doodling, and expression. Porcelain-topped whiteboard tables are a great option, as they clean easily and look very professional, but they can be quite expensive. Look for furniture or areas of the library that are currently underutilized, and consider turning those surfaces into whiteboards by repainting existing surfaces with whiteboard paint. Whiteboard paint can be used on a circulation desk, on a structural pole, on a smooth wall, on the endcaps of shelving units, and so on. At Stewart Middle Magnet School, Diana painted one wall in the makerspace with whiteboard paint, turning it into an active brainstorming area for students (see Figure 3.7).

Most traditional library tables have laminate wood tops that dry erase markers can be used on or whiteboard film can be added. Another option for writable surfaces is shower board, which can be sourced from home supply stores. This material can be cut up into individual whiteboards or mounted on a wall or table for an affordable writable surface. Be sure to provide plenty of high-quality dry erase markers for students to use; they're likely to go through them quickly.

Soft, Low Seating

It's important to support a variety of seating positions in an active learning space. At first, soft, low seating might not seem like an ideal option, considering that students are always on the go. However, this type of seating is perfect for students who need to take a break and take some time to reflect and process their ideas. They're excellent for brainstorming sessions as well. They also dampen noise, which can help to keep the space from becoming too loud. However, be careful not to err on the side of being too comfortable because this might cause students to feel less comfortable or willing to come up with new ideas or exchange leadership roles within groups (Doorley and Witthoft 2010, 44).

FIGURE 3.7 The Stewart Middle Magnet School whiteboard wall.

High Seating

Observe how students tend to work when not constrained by a traditional classroom setup. They will be constantly switching between sitting, perching, and walking. Offering multiple seating heights, including high seating, allows students to easily transition into what works best for them. Tall seating also has the advantage of lowering the amount of energy needed to switch from a seated to a standing position (Doorley and Witthoft 2010).

High seating options include bar stools and café-height tables. Students will perch while working on an idea or project and then quickly transition to the next task. In general, students probably won't be spending a long time in high seating, yet it is vital to supporting active learning and quick transitions. Be sure to invest in sturdy, durable options for high seating. Cheaper options often break quickly and can cause injury.

Seating That Supports Fidgeting

Many children (and adults) are kinesthetic learners. They need to have some sense of movement, or they cannot focus. Fidgeting can actually stimulate the brain and prevent mental fatigue (Cannon Design et al. 2010). Unfortunately, traditional classroom furniture tends to be stiff and rigid and doesn't allow for fidgeting without being disruptive. Be sure to include some dynamic seating options in the library that will allow students to move while they work. Think swivel chairs, chairs on wheels, and stools with uneven bases that allow for wobbling (as in Figure 3.8). Many teachers have found success with exercise balls, as they are very affordable and allow students to bounce slightly as they work.

FIGURE 3.8 Hokki stools at Stewart Middle Magnet School.

TRANSFORMING YOUR SPACE

There is great value in considering how environment

affects student learning experiences. But when it comes down to the practicalities, how does one go about transforming a space? Completely changing a library is rarely done overnight. Transforming a learning space takes thoughtful planning and observation. It is worth spending the time to observe how the space is used, communicate with all stakeholders, and visit other spaces for ideas and inspiration. Some changes are simple, quick, and affordable (e.g., rearranging the furniture, painting the walls, removing shelving). Often, such changes can make a big impact. Other transformations, such as replacing furniture or even building new spaces, requires finding funding sources. No matter what the budget, making a learning space more effective for students is very doable.

Planning a Library Transformation

If the goal is that the library space reflects the school community, it will be a vital asset to the school. The transformation will serve the needs of students, teachers, parents, and community members, so take the time to formulate a plan and get others involved in planning. When using a design thinking lens, it's important to gather ideas and research what your users want and need. Get their feedback early on in the process.

Be an Anthropologist

Before changing anything, start by observing how the space is currently used. Which ways do traffic patterns flow? Are there certain pieces of furniture that act as obstacles? Do students rearrange the furniture in a certain way? Where do students go when they want to read, work in groups, or have hands-on projects? How do teachers use the space? What happens when the space has to be set up for its various uses, such as whole-class use, small groups, presentations, special events, and so on? All of the data you gather at this stage will be invaluable when starting to plan the transformation.

Inclusive Strategies

As you observe your space, be sure to pay attention to how different groups of students use the space. Do you notice the female students gravitating more toward certain areas or activities? Are there areas that are too stimulating for students on the Autism spectrum? Does your space intentionally include and welcome students with a low socioeconomic status? Do you have tinkering height tables for all sizes of learners, including students in wheelchairs? Work to create a space that is inclusive of *all* your students.

Survey Your Community

Sullivan (2013) recommends taking the time to think about what types of information will be needed to plan the space when creating a needs assessment survey. Be careful to keep an open mind and avoid personal bias. Think about what types of problems are trying to be solved in transforming the space, and look at collected data with that in mind. It's best to build a survey primarily with closed-ended questions, as this will yield the most usable data.

Examples of Survey Questions

- What is the level of Internet and technology access students have outside of school?
- What types of environments do students most like to study in (coffee shop, with music, noisy, quiet, etc.)?
- In what types of hobbies and sports do your students engage?
- What technology, software, websites, and apps do students use for schoolwork and other activities?

It's also good to consider questions that can draw out students' learning styles, such as how they prefer to demonstrate understanding. Consider these examples:

- How do they like to spend their free time?
- What do they do for brain breaks?

The survey can be created with Google Forms or any other survey program and then systematically distributed to as many stakeholders as possible (Sullivan 2013).

Form a Focus Group

Create a focus group of students, teachers, and community members to help plan the transformation. Ideally, try to achieve a representative sampling of your school, such as selecting random students from an equal number of homerooms in each grade. Although it is easier to just work with volunteers, if you only go with people who choose to join voluntarily, you risk disenfranchising those who don't currently use the space.

Meet with your focus group in the space itself. Take a walking tour, and discuss what everyone is experiencing while walking around. Often, this will help you learn a great deal about how users experience the space. If possible, work through a challenge-based learning activity with the group as a whole. Identify what they are experiencing and how the space is being utilized as they

FIGURE 3.9   Lamar Middle School's in-progress project shelf.

work through the activity. After surveying the community, go over the results and discuss them with the focus group. As you continue to work through the planning and transformation process, this group will prove a vital resource for talking through ideas, dreaming up solutions, and turning those ideas into reality.

Managing an Active Learning Space

Managing an active learning space is not the same as managing a passive space. Deliberate organization and planning are key in helping to create a space where students can focus and be successful. The space should be set up in a way that inspires creativity and imagination, makes it easy for students to access the tools they need, and makes the procedures for putting things away clear. After the basics are established, a space like this can practically run itself.

Accessible Storage for In-Progress Projects

Students will rarely finish a project in the makerspace in one go. Challenge-based learning activities can often spread out over several weeks, and students need to have a space to store their projects when not using them. Consider creating an accessible storage space where students can independently put away and retrieve their projects, such as a wall of empty shelves (see Figure 3.9). Think of the space as a storage gallery, letting students see evidence of activity and ideas still in development (Doorley and Witthoft 2010). Special attention to storage is essential for those working with fixed and flexible scheduling in elementary libraries.

Create Clear Signage and Prompts

Signage is crucial in a well-functioning makerspace as it can help students understand where to put up supplies, how to store in-progress projects, and how to request materials. Label all storage items and color-code them when possible. Create design-prompt signage and display it throughout your space to encourage students who may be having trouble thinking up an idea. Try to be consistent in font and styling of the signs—this will help to brand the space and reduce visual noise (Doorley and Witthoft 2010).

Crowdfunding Larger Space Transformations

While the changes in the previous section were either easily affordable or free, eventually many of us want to move on to something bigger and create larger, lasting changes. Or we may want to make greater changes all at once rather than incrementally. Unless a librarian is lucky enough to have a renovation budget, creative sourcing of funds is key. There are many possible ways to go about this from crowdfunding to donations to grant-writing.

DonorsChoose

DonorsChoose (http://www.donorschoose.org) is a crowdfunding site specifically dedicated to education. Started in 2000 by a history teacher, DonorsChoose has grown to raise nearly $400 million to fulfill more than 600,000 classroom projects, funding everything from class sets of books to robotics kits to field trips to new furniture. Teachers create an account with DonorsChoose, create a wish list of items they'd like for their classroom, write an essay explaining how the materials will be used, and then solicit donations. At the time of this writing, DonorsChoose is only available to public school teachers.

This site can be a fantastic resource for those interested in utilizing challenge-based learning to acquire supplies and materials, and there are often matches available for projects involving science, technology, engineering, and mathematics (STEM); the arts; and maker activities. Because the scope of this chapter is on the learning environment, it's important to note that it is quite possible to raise funds for furniture and other physical space changes through DonorsChoose. At Ryan High School, for example, Colleen was able to raise funds for a Sound Booth/Digital Media Station, Girls Tech Camp, and Soldering Workshop. Aaron was able to purchase a 3D printer for his Denton High School library and even had school board members donate! At Stewart Middle Magnet School, funds were raised for both the Epic LEGO Wall and the paint for the whiteboard wall through DonorsChoose. Funds were also raised to purchase six Hokki stools (refer to Figure 3.8), which are chairs with uneven bottoms that allow students to wiggle and move. In addition to furniture and supplies purchased through DonorsChoose approved vendors, it is also possible to create projects with outside vendors. Note that this avenue does cost more points, and the teacher must have completed a successful project with approved vendors first. However, this can be a great option for furniture, paint, and other materials for space transformations that may not be readily available from approved vendors.

GoFundMe

GoFundMe (https://www.gofundme.com) is a crowdfunding site that is open to the general public. It is often used to help raise funds for special events, charities, medical expenses, and so on. GoFundMe can be an excellent resource for educators because you are allowed to keep all donations, whether or not you reach your goal. You can also make withdrawals while you are still raising money, allowing you to get started on your project immediately and work incrementally. There are no time limits on projects unless you choose to set them, and the fees taken from donations are minimal. One disadvantage of GoFundMe is that your donors are not guaranteed to receive a tax donation.

Grants

Crowdfunding is excellent for smaller scale projects, but many schools want to make larger changes all at once. If there is no district renovation budget, grants are the best options. Unfortunately, many grants specifically prohibit requesting furniture. Read the grant instructions carefully, and look for ways to tailor your project to the grantor's vision. Improved learning spaces can be tied to an increase in student achievement, an increase in community involvement, improved collaboration and independence in students, and so on. Discuss some of the improvements you've already made in your space and how this grant will continue to help them grow. If you're having trouble finding grants, try subscribing to an education grants listserv, and meet with your district's grant department. The money is out there; sometimes you just have to work harder to find it.

Make Changes Slowly

No matter what state your school library is currently in, it is absolutely possible to transform it into an active learning environment that will change the way your students experience school. Don't be afraid to start small and make changes incrementally—it took three years for Colleen to transform her middle school library. Be patient as you go through these changes as going slow can allow for big changes. At Lamar Middle School, Colleen had a student in a wheelchair who could not reach the circulation desk. Because the school was built before the Americans with Disabilities Act (ADA) compliance requirements, she began the process of an appeal to the district to get an ADA-compliant desk. It took two years for the process to be completed, but the wait was worth it. You will likely find that students and teachers will be excited about the changes. There may be some pushback, especially from those with a more traditional view of what a library should be. But as student engagement and use of the space increases, the naysayers will often decrease. Before you know it, your library will be welcomed into the 21st century with open arms.

Action Steps

- Be an anthropologist (observe, record, and survey students and teachers).
- Create a focus group.
- Organize a plan to include both quiet spaces and loud, active spaces.
- Prioritize your changes. What will make the most impact?
- Check into what kind of funding your district allows, and search for grant opportunities.

REFERENCES

Basye, Dale E., Peggy Grant, Stefanie Hausman, and Tod Johnston. 2015. *Get Active: Reimagining Learning Spaces for Student Success*. Eugene, OR: International Society for Technology in Education.

Cannon Design, VS Furniture, and Bruce Mau Design. 2010. *The Third Teacher: 79 Ways You Can Use Design to Transform Teaching & Learning*. New York: Abrams.

Doorley, Scott, and Scott Witthoft. 2010. *Make Space: How to Set the Stage for Creative Collaboration*. New York: Abrams.

Sullivan, Margaret L. 2013. *Library Spaces for 21st-Century Learners: A Planning Guide for Creating New School Library Concepts*. Chicago: American Association of School Librarians.

BIBLIOGRAPHY

Nair, Prakash, and Randall Fielding. 2005. *The Language of School Design: Design Patterns for 21st Century Schools*. Minneapolis, MN: DesignShare.

Thornburg, David. 2014. *From the Campfire to the Holodeck: Creating Engaging and Powerful 21st Century Learning Environments*. San Francisco: Jossey-Bass.

4

Workshop Model

We have to find a balance between open-ended, free-range exploration and guided learning in our makerspaces. It can be tricky to
figure out sometimes, but it's worth putting in the effort. A well-
crafted design challenge can inspire amazing creativity. Free-range
learning gives students opportunities for imaginative play. Both are
crucial for creating an environment where students can discover,
learn, and grow.

—Diana Rendina, media specialist, Stewart
Middle Magnet School

If you want to teach students a new skill in a small-group setting, you'll use
the workshop model. Working in this way allows you to schedule making and
have a set group of makers. This is an excellent method when resources are
low and you need to predetermine how many makers you can guide through
an activity. It can also be a great way to get started with makerspace activity
in your school if you're experiencing some pushback from teachers or administration because workshops can be done outside of structured class time (i.e.,
during lunch, recess, study hall, or after school).

BALANCING GUIDED INSTRUCTION AND TINKERING

Sometimes, you'll want to teach your students specific techniques or introduce them to a new maker resource. For this somewhat guided instruction,
you might decide to host a workshop in the library. If your students want to
learn to knit, for example, you'll host a workshop that shares the skills of knitting and purling. Yes, you might all work on the same scarf or project, which
seems counterintuitive in a makerspace, but the scarf is not the purpose of
the workshop. The purpose of the workshop is to give your students a new
skill set and teach them the basics so they can eventually go beyond the basics

and create something of their own invention. As Grace Lin points out in *The Art of Tinkering*, "The more traditional crafts you know, the more tools you have at your disposal when trying to make something new" (Wilkinson and Petrich 2014). By equipping our students with skill sets through guided workshops, we are empowering them to be able to create more things during open exploration.

Note that this is "guided" instruction, not direct instruction. Enlist knitting experts as mentors to aid students, give a few tips and pointers, and then hang back and stay nearby to make sure students can practice the skill you want them to learn. In this format, you are sharing how to do something and then seeing if your students can put those new ideas into their working memory and create something with their new skill set.

A workshop is also a great way to introduce a skill or a tool you want students to learn while incorporating a safety badging system. We'll discuss important safety tips later in this chapter.

Why a Workshop?

Depending on the group and the goals of their visit, it's sometimes important to guide workshops at first with a focus on providing more context and background information for the public before moving into inquiry and questioning. When staff members are not as experienced with facilitating tinkering, the workshop might end up more guided. The goal is ultimately to provide an environment where participants can explore, collaborate, and generate ideas and designs.
—Holly Arnason in *The Librarian's Guide to littleBits and STEAM*

A workshop gives students a new skill set and also builds their creative confidence. Although it seems counterintuitive that replicating a project would increase a student's potential creativity, replicating a project or an invention actually takes away the mysticism of invention. Learning how things work is a critical piece of what Jay Silver (co-inventor of Makey Makey) calls "invention literacy":

> Invention literacy is the ability to read and write human made stuff, from toasters to apps. People think inventors perform magic, but invention is no more magical than reading and writing a sentence. There is a grammar to inventing from mechanical tools, to design thinking, coding, and beyond. There is a literature of inventions, from bicycles to televisions, all around us to draw inspiration from. Just as Thoreau read Emerson's writings, so too did Edison read Tesla's inventions.[1]

By hosting workshops and teaching students new skills, you will inspire students to experiment and get creative. Without some instruction and guidance, students might get frustrated and give up. Following a simple project

---

1. This and all subsequent Jay Silver quotes are from a telephone interview by the author on July 27, 2016.

will actually build upon students' prior skill sets and give them the building blocks to apply what they've learned toward creating their own inventions.

For example, Colleen hosted a sewing circuit workshop with an expert on hand. The students experienced many mistakes and setbacks, but by having a sewing expert available, they were able to persevere through their mistakes and learn from these small failures. Without an expert, they might have given up. In this workshop, Colleen had a group of girls come for an after-school tech camp to learn to sew circuits. Many of these girls had no sewing skills and no knowledge of circuitry. They made many mistakes, and many students did not have enough time to finish their projects. Instead of leaving them all to finish on their own, she hosted a second workshop where she could help students individually by allowing them to come in during their free time or during open make time. One student in particular had to completely redo her work, which is something quite common in a makerspace project *and* a sewing project. She was very frustrated, but by having a facilitator there to guide her, she was able to decode the mistakes in her first attempt and learn more about circuitry in the process.

By taking her project apart and redoing it, she realized how parallel circuits work, and she became more effective in her sewing skills. She went home to work further and came back the next day for a battery. When she placed the battery in and flipped the switch, all of her LEDs lit up along with her smile. If Colleen had not held the second workshop, this student wouldn't have finished her work, but more importantly, she wouldn't have debugged her project and made the connections about how parallel circuits are created.

> **Guidelines and instructions are not the enemy of makerspaces. Working through guided projects can help students to develop the skills that they need to further explore creatively. It's true that some students can just figure it out, but most need that gentle push to get them started.**
> **—Diana Rendina, media specialist, Stewart Middle Magnet School**

These workshops focused on adding skills to our students' maker toolbox give them a chance to learn with an expert nearby, thus lessening their frustration and strengthening their decoding and debugging skills.

Brainstorming Ideas for Workshops

You might develop themes for workshop ideas before school starts, but you shouldn't set up an entire schedule of workshops because you need to base your workshops on your students' ideas and desires. You can do this by asking the students what they want to create. If you want to plan ahead, instead of deciding what your students will create, come up with goals and objectives you want them to meet. Maybe you want them to have more hands-on experience with building creations with their own hands, or maybe you want them to develop a specific skill set for an upcoming design challenge.

Colleen knew that she wanted her students to be able to fix things that break and to be able to start inventing with electronics. To obtain those goals, she

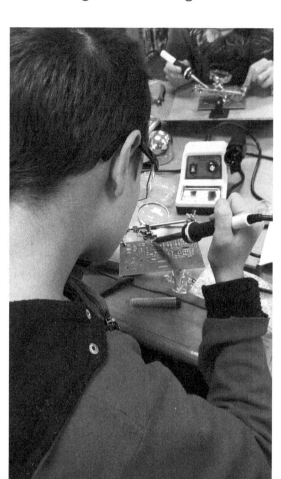

FIGURE 4.1   Intro to Soldering workshop.

knew the students needed to learn to solder. The students were very excited to learn, but she didn't have the tools or the expertise. Luckily, Colleen had visited her local makerspaces and made maker connections, as referenced in Chapter 2. She partnered with the public library and technology librarian, Trey Ford, to give students these new skills so they would be able to fix broken headphones or begin making basic electronic projects and later more complicated electronics, robots, and so on. This workshop also gave them some important safety training regarding using a soldering iron, plus they made a cool Makey badge they were able to keep (see Figure 4.1).

Beginning and Advanced Workshops

Keep in mind that one workshop might inspire another more advanced workshop. At Ryan High School, the students enjoyed the initial soldering workshop so much that they asked for an advanced soldering workshop. Colleen put the students in charge of picking out project ideas, and they found an FM Radio Kit they wanted to build. Now these makers learned not only about soldering but also about the components of an FM radio and how a radio is put together, which will further aid them in becoming more invention literate. Plus, this advanced workshop solidified the students' expertise in safely using a soldering iron. Therefore, after students attended this workshop, they passed a skill set level and were allowed to "check out" the soldering stations for use in the library.

Even though workshops are based on what students want to create, you also need to make sure the projects students choose are doable. Do your students have the skills it takes to complete the project they want to create? Will the project be executable in the time frame you have available for the students? When Diana Rendina's students requested a sewn circuit workshop, they were eager to get started with their project. And yet in the first meeting, Diana

FIGURE 4.2 Student circuit bracelets.

quickly realized that most of these students had never even threaded a needle and sewn a button. Thus, for the first workshop, the first goal became to successfully sew a few buttons onto a felt bracelet (Figure 4.2). After students had accomplished that, a second workshop was scheduled to delve into the circuits.

In the case of the FM Radio Kits, Trey Ford (public librarian) and Colleen found that while the project was a great way to practice soldering, it was more labor intensive than the students were ready to tackle. Many students still persevered and finished their radios, but remember that one reason we have a facilitator in the library is to help make guided decisions. While you should let your students choose ideas for workshops, you still need to make sure students have the skill set needed to complete the desired project so you can maximize your time and your school resources.

Sources for Workshop Ideas

Other ways to brainstorm workshop ideas are to keep an eye on Twitter and chat with other librarians. You might even host a workshop based on something like #LEGOtinkering or art robots where the skill students are honing is the ability to tinker or an exploration of materials. You can also show your students project books and talk with your students to see what types of projects they are interested in making.

Remember that, as the librarians, we are the facilitators of our spaces. Just as we might recommend a book that we know a student will love, we should also seek out projects and ideas that will be beneficial for our students. Sometimes, there might be an activity that our students haven't shown an interest in (yet), but we know they'll love it after they dig in. Don't worry; they'll be quick to let you know whether or not they like it.

Inclusive Strategies

Workshops are an excellent opportunity to work closely with groups of students who traditionally can be disenfranchised in larger groups. Diana held several workshops with her STEMgirls club, which is a girls-only maker club that she started with several other teachers at her school. By having the makerspace and tools to themselves during these workshops, the girls opened up and were unafraid to express themselves creatively.

Product-Specific Workshops

Sometimes, you might want to host a workshop focused around a product you already have so that you can get students interested in your resources. For instance, let's say you have littleBits, and you want students to be more inventive with them. You have to think about how you can teach students to see the potential that each Bit module holds.

Colleen tackled this problem when students at Ryan were constantly messing about with littleBits but seemed to want some guidance. She decided to hold a synth workshop to teach students about each synth piece. As she was writing *The Librarian's Guide to littleBits and STEAM* (Graves 2016), she'd chatted with academic librarian Chad Mairn about his own littleBits Synth workshop. She was able to learn from him and use his workshop model to teach her high school students how to make their own analog synthesizer with littleBits. (See how she organized Bits for this in Figures 4.3 and 4.4.) This very fun and focused workshop allowed students to explore specific soundscapes and learn about sound and sine waves, all while learning how

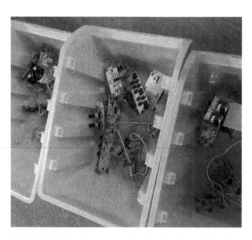

FIGURE 4.3 Sorted Synth Bits for the workshop.

to use this new resource. One student was able to transfer that new learning into creepy sound effects for a littleBits movie that another group of students was working on.

Tips for Hosting Workshops

We've had workshops during lunch, after school, and even before school with attendance varying from 5 to 75 students! The important thing to consider before hosting a maker-space workshop is to know your boundaries. How many kids can you handle in the space at one time? How complicated is the project you will be working on? If the project is something simple, you might be able to handle teaching 75 students at once. However, if it is a very intricate

FIGURE 4.4 Sorted Synth Bits for each participant in the workshop.

process, you may want to limit your numbers to a group of fewer than 10. If you have many students interested but need to limit your numbers, consider staggering and repeating workshops. In addition, you can bring in additional facilitators, such as other teachers, public librarians, or parents, who are familiar with the skill set you're teaching.

At Lamar, so many students wanted to make brushbots, that Colleen had to have repeat Maker Monday sessions. Over the course of a month, she held repeat workshops so that all of the students who wanted to learn to make simple robots would get a chance to attend. By repeating the workshop multiple times, more than 100 students were able to tinker with her restricted supplies that would only allow for 20 students to make brushbots during a single session. Students took brushbots apart after each session so that they could be reused for the next workshop.

At the high school level initial soldering workshop, Colleen held sessions during lunch and limited attendance to 10 students for each lunch period. By repeating the workshop over two days with public librarian Trey as the mentor expert, 80 students from Ryan High School were able to add beginning soldering to their skill toolbox.

Choosing Participants

Create a sign-up sheet and advertise each workshop well in advance. Allow students to sign up at the circulation desk, on the library door, by responding via a Remind text, or by simply filling out a Google Form on the library web page. Find what works for you and your students. When Colleen was at middle school, she could advertise her Maker Monday workshops on Instagram. At

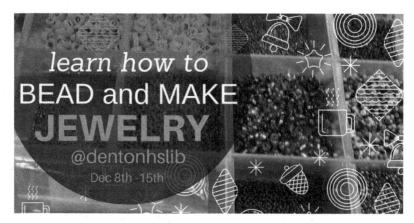

FIGURE 4.5   Flyer for jewelry-making workshop.

the high school level, the best advertisement is word of mouth and hosting workshops during lunch. Students show up in the library and ask, "What are we making today?" because they are already in the library for lunch and often their friends pressure them to join in learning new things.

Consumables vs. Reusable

When designing workshops, you'll also have to decide ahead of time if you are going to reuse materials, or if students will be allowed to take items home. Students will ask every time! This should be decided based on the cost of the product, how the product was purchased, how long the item will hold interest, and if you consider it consumable or not. While brushbots are relatively low cost, Colleen felt that students would lose interest in the make rather quickly after they got the bots home, so students took apart the brushbot elements and organized them for the next group to use. High-cost items such as Makey Makey and littleBits are not consumable, and students may need to pass skill level tests so that they can check them out to take home (as one would a book or other resource), but these items always have to be returned. Other consumable items, such as paper circuit and sewing circuit supplies, should be figured into your budget or purchased through crowdfunding. Because the supplies for Diana's STEMgirls project were purchased through DonorsChoose, the students were able to take home their circuit bracelets after the workshop.

Inclusive Strategies

Following are great ways to get girls involved in maker-focused workshops:

- Let girls become mentors for other students.
- Make time for girls (set aside time for girls-only maker workshops).

- Combine high-tech and low-tech activities (e.g., sewing and circuits).
- Craft workshops where problem-solving is sprinkled with creativity ("Can you design the circuitry to light up this drawing?").

INTRODUCING NEW SKILLS AND SAFETY STANDARDS

If students need to learn something as dangerous as soldering or as intricate as jewelry making, a workshop focused on basic safety standards might be the perfect event. Teaching safety is just like teaching any concept; judge the class accordingly and teach them at their level for each required tool. Have students complete a needs and skills assessment to see which kids are experts and which kids will require more hands-on training. When teaching tool safety, there is a fine line between fear and respect for the tool. What further complicates this instruction is that this fine line is different for every kid (and every tool). Creating a badging system or categorizing tools by safety skill may help with organization and safety precautions. Some participatory stations might require rules or standards like this example of rules Colleen has posted at her "Take Apart Stations":

Take Apart Rules

1. Don't Force anything.
2. Always use the right tools.
3. Be safe! Wear gloves if needed.
4. Go slow.
5. Don't break anything.
6. Challenge yourself: Can you put it back together, and it be in working condition?

Respecting Tools

Balance respect (for tools) without scaring the kids.
—Oren Connell, Ann Richards School for Young Women Leaders[2]

Oren Connell manages the makerspace at Ann Richards School for Young Women Leaders, an all-girls public school serving grades 6–12 in Austin, Texas. In addition to making sure the band saw blade is always sharp, "Mr. Oren" works with students during school hours and after school to inform, train, and encourage a wide variety of projects and processes from laser cutters to

2. This and all subsequent Oren Connell quotes are from a telephone interview by the author on July 27, 2016.

hot glue guns. Oren collaborates closely with Ann Richards faculty to encourage, train, and facilitate maker and STEAM-focused projects (science, technology, engineering, arts, and mathematics) in the classroom. While interviewing Oren for this book, we spoke at length about teaching students to respect tools. During their first year of implementing a makerspace at Ann Richards, Oren focused on needs assessment for training. He trained all students and staff in safety at Ann Richards during their second year rollout of the makerspace. For the next year, he's going to focus on teaching students on an "as needed" basis and/or per teacher request for classroom instruction.

When teaching students a new tool, Oren noticed that in some cases there might be one fearful kid whose fear may spread to the others in the group. In this scenario, you don't want fear of the tool to spread to other students, so you focus on lessening the fear of the tool and strengthening the respect for the tool. On the other hand, an overconfident student with a general disregard for safety may require explicit instruction on what students should fear in regard to this particular tool (e.g., the hot tip of a soldering iron and the damage it can do) while still instilling a healthy respect for the tool.

Badging or Skill Rating System

Andy Plemmons, maker librarian featured in Chapter 6, had some other great ideas for using workshops to introduce tools and tool safety. He enumerated how partnering with Gretchen Thomas at the University of Georgia (UGA) has helped his students learn how to use certain tools in his elementary makerspace. Gretchen is an instructor at UGA in the Department of Career and Information Studies. She has developed a course called "Maker Dawgs" (the bulldog is the UGA mascot). She is under a larger STEAM initiative in her department called Project Spark. In this semester-long course, students read *Invent to Learn*, explore maker tools, and visit Andy's school to help each week on Tuesdays and Thursdays. At the beginning of the semester, Andy gives these awesome mentors ideas on how to help, but over the course of the semester, the UGA students start designing their own projects for the elementary students. This year, the whole class will be taught on Andy's campus, and he's hoping they create a badging system where students earn a badge when they explore a certain tool. Eventually, the kids come up with projects. Andy notes that when working with off-campus mentors, it is imperative to teach these mentors how to work with students and how to facilitate learning, that is, not do all the work for the students.

For older students such as Oren's students at Ann Richards, consider implementing a skill rating system. For instance, you could rate your tools by skill level. Category 1 would be tools that students can use without any safety training (but may require a smidge of direct instruction) such as Makey Makey, littleBits, and Sphero. Category 2 tools require some safety training but will not require a teacher after student has the basic safety training, such as paper circuits, sewing circuit supplies, and smaller electronics. Category 3 tools would require specific training or workshop attendance and a teacher's permission to use tools, such as soldering stations, drills, miter saws, and so on.

Oren also notes it is important to hang signage for protection. In his space, students are reminded to put their hair up and out of the way, wear headphones for hearing protection, and wear safety glasses.

Workshops for Safety Skills

You may base a workshop on teaching students how to use a tool so that you can train them on the safety standards for that tool. Colleen learned that Oren offered the same Makey badge workshop to teach his students the very basics of soldering. This is Oren's preferred way to train students for safety standards as it encourages engagement and gives them something physical to show for their accomplishment.

Remember, a workshop's focus is to give students a new skill set so they will be successful when you issue a challenge. This new skill set will allow them to attempt to solve the challenge or discover new learning that will add to their inventor's toolbox. These skills allow them to "make meaning" that adds to their invention literacy toolbox.

Because your design challenges are also based on student ideas, a workshop might even spark a new challenge. This is what happened when Colleen's students chatted with Diana's students about building brushbots and ended the conversation by challenging Diana's students to create catapults (as discussed in Chapter 2).

Training as Needed vs. Whole-Class Instruction

A makerspace is not just glorified shop class.
—Oren Connell, teacher at Ann Richards School

This year, students will come in for training on an as-needed basis at Ann Richards School. Oren created a shop manual based on all the tools available in his makerspace. He hangs the manual for each tool near the specified tool so that kids can pick up a new skill when they need it. When a student asks for help with a tool that they could easily learn without assistance, Oren can literally hand his students the learning by handing them his manual. When students decide they need training on a new tool with a higher skill level that requires teacher assistance, they will read up on the tool in Oren's shop manual, and then take an online assessment over the tool they want to train on. If they pass the assessment, they will schedule a training with Oren (or another qualified teacher).

Because, as Oren says, "Some kids just want to absorb everything! They will learn everything just to learn," he is planning some hands-on training to get kids in the door via workshops. These workshops will help kids gain new skills through simple projects such as creating Mother's Day cards on the laser cutter. After the students are trained, they will get a button featuring the tool. Plus, he offers basic safety training for all students and specific tool training as needed, via a workshop or as a class per teacher request.

Skill Levels at Ann Richards School

- Level 1: You've used it, but still need close adult supervision.
- Level 2: You've used it enough that it doesn't need "close" supervision, but you still have to get permission, and a teacher must be in the room.
- Level 3: Advanced—You've used it right so many times, you don't have to get permission to use it, but a teacher must be in the room.
- Trainer: You've used it so many times that you are no longer a student of the tool but are now a trainer who can teach others. (Oren notes that this is mostly achieved by students in regard to teaching others how to use the laser cutter and the 3D printer.)

MENTOR EXPERTS

One of the challenges with facilitating a makerspace is teaching the students a wide variety of skills sets, even though you as the facilitator may not have those particular skills. The best way to offer a plethora of workshops is to reach out to your school community and local community makers. You hopefully met experts when you ventured out and visited local makerspaces and Maker Faires (or maybe you even sent out an expertise survey for your parents and found expert makers in this way).

Community Experts

Aaron Graves wanted his high school students to learn to knit even though he doesn't have the ability to knit and purl. Instead of skipping out on offering the workshop, he checked with faculty at his school to see if anyone could

FIGURE 4.6 Knitting flyer.

help teach his students how to knit. He had an overwhelming response of knitting mentor volunteers! Many teachers came down during their own lunch to help students learn to knit, and because he'd sent a request out to his staff, teachers even came down to learn (Figure 4.6).

If you cannot find an expert in your school community, check with your local community. You can maximize your student's learning by partnering with mentor experts who reside in your community. Colleen didn't feel like her soldering skills were adequate to host a workshop, so she invited public librarian Trey to her school. With his help, she was able to offer soldering workshops. In return, she volunteered to teach sewing circuit workshops at the public library.

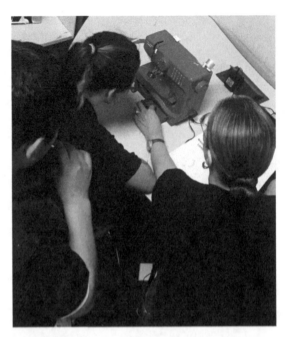

FIGURE 4.7 Parent volunteer teaching sewing.

When Diana received some sewing machines for her makerspace through DonorsChoose, she had many students eager to learn. However, she quickly realized that the best way for students to learn how to use them was through one-on-one instruction, and she wasn't always able to provide that herself. One of the parents of an after-school makers club member volunteered to come in and teach interested students how to sew. She was able to work individually with the students, freeing up Diana to continue facilitating other maker projects with the other students in the club (Figure 4.7).

Global Experts

Looking outside of your school to the global community is another great way to find experts. Reach out on Twitter, look through Skype in the Classroom, or sign up for a system such as Nepris that allows you to contact experts to chat with your students. In 2016, Colleen ran a girls' tech camp at her high school and invited Jie Qi, the inventor of the Chibitronics LED stickers and accompanying paper circuit notebook, to chat with her female students about designing paper circuits. By chatting with this expert, Colleen's students were able to learn tips about crafting paper circuits that they would never have gained from reading a book or following a tutorial. Instead, they had a real expert share her expertise and increase their paper circuit building skills. The students learned more about paper circuits in the one-hour chat with Jie than Colleen learned in a year of tinkering with paper circuits!

Sparking Design Challenges

Many times, workshops and mentor experts are great springboards to design challenges. A design challenge can really help give your makers a theme to focus on while still being open ended and allowing students to make what they desire. While it may seem that guiding what students make is counterintuitive to a makerspace, this type of focused learning can actually help students grow creatively. These creative constraints also help students develop invaluable problem-solving skills. (Chapter 5 will cover creative constraints in more depth.) By introducing a themed design challenge, students have to problem-solve to create something that answers the challenge, but they are not given direct instructions on how to solve the challenge.

Action Steps

- Survey your students to determine what types of skills and projects they are interested in.
- Talk to parents, teachers, and community members to find local maker mentors.
- Determine what safety skills should be taught for your space.
- Consider creating a badging or skill-rating system for the tools in your space.

REFERENCES

Graves, Colleen. 2016. *The Librarian's Guide to LittleBits and STEAM.* New York: LittleBits.

Rendina, Diana. "The Value of Guided Projects in Makerspaces." *Renovated Learning.* January 18, 2016. http://renovatedlearning.com/2016/01/18/value-guided-projects-makerspaces.

Wilkinson, Karen, and Mike Petrich. 2014. *The Art of Tinkering: Meet 150 Makers Working at the Intersection of Art, Science & Technology.* San Francisco: Weldon Owen.

BIBLIOGRAPHY

Graves, Colleen. "What Age Is Best? LittleBits STEAM Student Set Review Part II." *Create, Collaborate, Innovate.* March 11, 2016. https://colleengraves.org/2016/03/11/what-age-is-best-littlebits-student-steam-set-review-part-ii.

Graves, Colleen. "Nation of Makers." *Create Collaborate Innovate.* June 18, 2016. https://colleengraves.org/2016/06/18/nationofmakers-family-project-take-apart-and-rebuild-toys.

Martinez, Sylvia Libow, and Gary Stager. 2013. *Invent to Learn: Making, Tinkering, and Engineering in the Classroom.* Torrance, CA: Constructing Modern Knowledge Press.

5

Introduction to Design Thinking, Design Challenges, and Crowdsourced Research Methods

Open exploration and guided workshops are fantastic ways to encourage tinkering, exploration, and inquiry in students. Design thinking, design challenges, and crowdsourcing research methods will help students to dive deep into making and to think like designers. These strategies have the power to get students' creative juices flowing and help them to structure their making in a way that allows them to be more reflective and to see making integrated with real-world applications.

DESIGN THINKING AND THE DESIGN PROCESS

It begins with tapping into student curiosity and allowing them to create, test, and re-create until they eventually launch what they've made to a real audience.
—John Spencer and A. J. Juliani, *LAUNCH*

Design thinking is a human-centered approach to creative problem-solving. In *LAUNCH: Using Design Thinking to Boost Creativity and Bring Out the Maker in Every Student*, Spencer and Juliani describe design thinking as "a way to think about creative work. It starts with empathy working to really understand the problems people are facing before attempting to create solutions" (2016, 24). When students incorporate design thinking into making, the process can look different for different projects. In general, design thinking covers a student's or group's ability to identify a problem, research the problem and research solutions, generate a multitude of human-centered ideas to solve the problem, prototype ideas, improve ideas, and own failure by learning from it and hammering on. This process allows students to experience a growth mindset from persevering through making. Design thinking also allows for students to have more than one right answer to a problem because it focuses on "the creative genius of students" (Spencer and Juliani 2016, 25). Design thinking is process heavy, so even if students don't end up with a working project in the end, that is okay because the journey and the process are more important than the end product.

Design Thinking

Many designers create things without thinking of a real need. That is why design thinking is so important. Because it is a human-based approach to design, it focuses on finding solutions to real problems that people encounter. Consider a teacher who wants to redesign a classroom to meet students' needs. If the teacher interviews students to see what they want in a classroom environment, then the teacher is using design thinking. In this way, the teacher is researching user needs. To go further, the teacher might take the problems the students have with the current classroom design and research other school and classroom solutions to this problem. Before completely changing the classroom design, the teacher might create visual layouts or prototype models to once again show the classroom users. If students dislike something about a prototype, the teacher doesn't give up, but rather works on improving ideas based on the student feedback. The design process is an integral part of design thinking.

Inclusive Strategies

Empathy is a huge part of design thinking. For your next project, look into using design thinking to have your students design something for a group that is different from them. An example might be creating a contraption to help children in third-world countries carry water to their home. This gives your students an opportunity to look at the world from the perspective of someone else.

Design Process

The design process is part of design thinking, but there are differences to note. Whereas the design process might be used to activate design thinking, the design process also can be used without thinking of basic human needs. The actual design process has its basis in engineering, so there is less of an emphasis on empathy and more on the process of coming up with and testing a design

(Figure 5.1). The Science Buddies website lays out the engineering design process as follows: (1) define the problem; (2) do background research; (3) specify requirements; (4) brainstorm, evaluate, and choose a solution; (5) develop and prototype the solution; (6) test the solution; (7) determine whether or not the solution meets the requirements; (8) based on results and data, go back, redesign the prototype, and test and evaluate again; (9) communicate the results (Science Buddies 2016). This process is not always linear and often involves creating many iterations before the final solution is reached. So, you can see how these two concepts—design process and design thinking—might get confused; instead,

FIGURE 5.1 Student using a design process worksheet.

think of the design process as part of design thinking. One is a process and design thinking is a way of using that process to focus on actual human needs.

Implementing Design Thinking into Student Projects

When looking for problems or challenges that need to be solved, the idea for a problem can come from either the student or the teacher. You may decide as the facilitator that you'd like to frame the learning by identifying the problem. You'll read about one of our case studies in Chapter 8 in which the teacher provided the framework for the problem she wanted students to solve. Or, you may decide that you want students to identify problems they want to solve. The important aspect to teaching students how to think like designers is to teach them how to "gather data" to solve problems. In Kristin Fontichiaro's book, *Design Thinking*, she discusses quantitative and qualitative data and explains that "in design thinking, we focus mostly on qualitative data—the words and actions of the real people who will interact with your inventions" (2015, 10). In other words, this type of research focuses more on opinions, which is quite the opposite of traditional research that generally relies more on quantitative data. Teach your students to make careful observations when trying to incorporate human-centered design. After all, the point of this type of design is not to point out what we know, but to find what is or can be helpful to others. In our library makerspaces, we encourage our students to interview others, make phone calls to corporations and experts, and crowdsource their research to gather this type of qualitative data.

Because we are relying on qualitative data, it is important to teach students how to crowdsource their research methods, and the best way is for them to ask for information from others. Fontichiaro stresses the importance of teaching students good interview techniques because students will naturally come up with leading questions. Therefore, we need to instruct our students on how to write interview questions that ask the opinions and feelings of others without implying them.

As a teacher librarian that functions as an instructional partner on a school campus, your focus should be on how you can use this method to incorporate real world or authentic research into your library makerspace. During the design thinking process, students will gather lots and lots of information (or research) and then have to sort through that information to help create a solution. Sorting through the data can be a messy but rewarding experience. In Fontichiaro's book, she suggests creating an "affinity wall" or a large blank wall where students can gather sticky notes of ideas. She suggests "clustering data" as a means to help organize the chaos (2015, 17–18). Spencer and Juliani have a similar phase in the Launch Cycle that they call "Navigate ideas" based on "ideating" and "whiteboarding" (2016, 57) It is important in both methods to let students visualize ideas on a large scale, be it a large post-it note wall of ideas or a smaller collaborative scale such as a vision board.

Making and playing with design helps people learn how things are made and how they work. Even if students don't end up designing software for a living, chances are they will work with someone who does. What can design thinking do for the workforce? Consider a library assistant who works in circulation. He or she has some basic programming skills in Scratch designing games. The library assistant takes time to meet with circulation software developers to work on the challenge of making improvements to the library's circulation software. A potential problem with the software they use everyday might be that you have to manually move the cursor from the patron search window to the item search window. A library assistant with some experience writing code who knows about "if-then" statements might realize that an if-then statement could be written to make the software recognize the length of digits in a patron barcode and move to the patron search box. The same thing could happen for an item barcode, and suddenly the conversation is much richer and potentially more beneficial for all because of shared languages and experiences.

DESIGN CHALLENGES

It seems contradictory, but when it comes to creative work, limitations mean freedom.

—Austin Kleon, *Steal Like an Artist*

When first introduced to the concept of design challenges in makerspaces, many educators start to picture classes where every student is required to build an identical project following a specific set of instructions. Stager and Martinez (2013) often refer to this as the "20 birdhouses" effect, where every student in the class follows directions and creates an identical birdhouse. But as Kleon (2012) points out beautifully, creating limitations and guidelines can actually offer creative freedom. By utilizing design challenges with our students, we can help them to get past the overwhelming question of "what do I make next?" and offer them a specific goal to focus on.

Creative Constraint and Blank Page of Paper Syndrome

What initially seems like a constraint or limitation can, in fact, foster new forms of creativity.
—Mitchel Resnick et al., *Design Principles for Tools*
to Support Creative Thinking

Amos Blanton, Senior LEGO Idea Studio Manager at the LEGO Foundation, says that when designing activities to introduce children to new tools, it is okay to start with some constraints as this will help makers avoid the "blank page" syndrome.[1] Like writer's block, a blank page, or a project with no constraint, can be "intimidating for students because they will not know where to start." By constraining the activity in some way, it challenges the student and gives them a place to begin. Blanton reiterates that the activity you design should "invite students to tinker and take one step beyond their comfort zone." Blanton adds:

> As a facilitator, the end-goal is for students to learn to define their own structure and constraints that encourage creativity. As a maker, students should become more comfortable with tools and materials. Once that comfort level is reached, your job is to encourage more and more freedom for students to choose what to make and gradually invite your makers to set their own direction.

When designing these creative constraints, it is important to focus on creating prompts that will encourage students to tinker and create, rather than shut down their creative process. Resnick et al. (2005) discusses the concept this way: "In designing creativity support tools, we put a high priority on tinkerability—we want to encourage users to mess with the materials, to try out multiple alternatives, to shift directions in the middle of the process, to take things apart and create new versions."

As artistic educators, we can delve even further into the open-ended concept by looking at Jay Silver's (co-inventor of Makey Makey) thesis of the "world as a construction kit."[2] Silver maintains the importance of realizing that a project has many parts and that the real creativity begins when educators look at

---

1. This and all subsequent Amos Blanton quotes are from a telephone interview by the author on July 27, 2016.
2. This and all subsequent Jay Silver quotes are from a telephone interview by the author on July 26, 2016.

creating open-beginning and open-middle parts to the project. We do not have to make all projects open-ended, but rather look at all aspects of a project (prologue, beginning, middle, end, epilogue) and constrain projects at different times for different purposes when designing creative constraints. Silver says, "Open endedness is great, but people don't realize that projects have many parts, and projects can be more or less specified in all of those segments." When crafting these design prompts, it is important for educators to "take a step back and consider how to open the project up in an interesting way or realize the project is too loose and realize they need to close part of the project to help create creative constraints to motivate students to explore passionate ends."

Silver also emphasizes that this structure helps educators create "context to help you think." One way of looking at creating an open beginning, middle, and end for a creative project is to see the world as Silver sees it—as a construction kit with three main categories: tools, materials, and containers. He gives this example to explain:

> Consider the world as a paint construction kit: where the tool is a paintbrush, the loose material is the paint, and the container is the canvas (or the place where your painting goes). An open-ended project is one where you don't specify what someone is painting. Instead you give them the paint construction kit and say paint what comes to mind. In an open-beginning project, you give them tools and a container, but no paint. In an open-middle project, you give them paint, but no paintbrush. Makers would end up painting with leaves, stamp paint with tools, etc.

However, it's important for educators to realize that instruction and scaffolding is still needed. Silver suggests including scaffolding in all parts of the project:

> If your project is open-ended, you may want to have a closed beginning or closed middle. In the real world, designers don't just look at the world and decide to make a certain product; instead, they start out with various constraints that they impose through an artistic process. Kids don't have that skill set yet, so we have to give them some constraints. Projects don't just have ends, so educators can look into creating open starting points or open middles and close off different aspects of the project as a way to creatively constrain students.

By "playing with the closed and open parts of the project" educators can "create new fields of creative art with this structure."

If students are creating projects with materials and tools, the tools may correspond with the parts of the project. Silver gives the anecdote of asking a class to paint the *Mona Lisa* (a closed-ended project), but instead of having just a closed end, he suggests giving the students an open middle by giving them paintbrushes, canvases, and the prompt to paint the *Mona Lisa*—but not giving them paint. Students will have to explore what material they would like to use as paint instead. By creating an open middle, students will play with the concept of paint, and maybe "students will paint with strawberry juice or paint with cheerios." This open middle gives students a creative constraint and a chance to figure out how to make (or problem-solve how to create) paint when they are not provided with paint.

If you take the tools, container, materials, and open one of them, then you get a vast world of possibilities.
—Jay Silver, founder/CEO of JoyLabz/Makey Makey

Design Challenges vs. Design Thinking

A design challenge is simply a "can you do this?" challenge put forth to makers to give them a focus with time constraints. A challenge gives students a direct problem to solve with creative ideas and is a great way to get students to work collaboratively. Makey Makey co-inventor Jay Silver states that, "Design challenges are so important . . . it introduces time limits, a focused theme, and ends with a show and tell."

Although design challenges *can be* based on design thinking, they don't have to be. For example, our Makey Makey Challenge was a straight design challenge: "How can you create a custom game and game controller with Makey Makey?" If we decided to introduce design thinking as an aspect in this challenge, we could add, "How can you create a custom game controller for a stroke victim utilizing a Makey Makey?" or "Interview someone about how you could improve a controller for their favorite game." One is focused on fun and the other is focused on designing for a specific human need. Both are good ways to challenge our students to think like designers. Some of our research project examples in Chapter 8 are design thinking focused and based on social action if you want to read more about human-centered design and research.

Why Design Challenges?

Students enjoy a challenge. For example, Colleen challenged her high school BLAST (a class designed around Building Leadership And Strengths Together) students to create an obstacle course for Sphero robots and create a program for Sphero to drive the course. This design challenge was a huge collaborative effort that extended from one class to the next. The introductory class discussed function over fun and created a basic course with tape to test Sphero programming during their design process. The next class added dimensionality to the course with cardboard and other recyclables on hand. This led to an interesting ramp shooting out of the base of one of the library tinkering tables.

The last class over the course of two days was trying to fix all the design flaws of the course and had trouble getting Sphero to jump safely out of a cardboard tube. One student became fixated on building a swing for Sphero so that it could roll out of the tube, into the swing, and then be gently placed to the ground. This particular student had often been a lurker in the makerspace but did not always actively engage in making. This design challenge and collaborative problem-solving gave him maker fever, and when the class broke for lunch, he stayed to continue ideating and improving his design.

This problem of building an obstacle course for Sphero challenged him to think outside of his normal making routine. His actual design took him a very long time, but his idea ended up being amazingly simple after he tweaked his thinking. After he got Sphero through the obstacle course on his K'nex and cardboard swing, he started shouting, "Yes! Yes! I did it! I made a contraption and it works! After so many fails!"

Reflecting on this design challenge, we can ask ourselves a few questions. How does this type of learning engage students? How does it help them learn to problem-solve? How does it help them become innovators? Without the problem created by the other students of incorporating the table base and ramp into the group's design, would this student still have made this invention?

METHODS FOR DEVELOPING DESIGN CHALLENGES

Framing a problem with a design challenge that students need to creatively address is the best way to get students tinkering instead of just making by number.
—David Saunders from *The Librarian's Guide to littleBits and STEAM*

Design challenges can be simple or complex. They can last for weeks or for less than an hour. And their effectiveness is often determined by the forethought and planning that goes into designing and developing them. This section will take a look at some best practices to consider when planning a design challenge—from crafting the prompt to facilitating student learning during a challenge. In addition, the next two chapters will offer some elementary and secondary design challenges for you to try with your students.

Design Challenge Best Practices

Although there is certainly no one-size-fits-all model for developing a design challenge, there are best practices to consider that can help effectively plan a challenge for students. By reflecting on these practices while shaping design challenge prompts and preplanning before executing design challenges in the library, you can help facilitate a dynamic learning experience that will keep students engaged.

David Saunders is a middle school library media specialist and library coordinator living in southwestern Connecticut. He is a Google Certified Innovator, Trainer, and Administrator, Raspberry Pi Certified Educator, littleBits Global Chapter Leader, CUE Rockstar faculty member, and CUE SteamPunk advisor. He suggests giving students "open-ended prompts, like *Build Something that Draws Something*, and then instill creative confidence in his students by telling them, 'Trust yourself; there is no right answer. Instead focus on what the questions are that we need to ask to find a solution.' This gets students tinkering instead of just making by number" (Graves 2015).

Elements for a Successful Design Challenge

- Challenge by topic or materials:
  - Limitations: Build something that moves with littleBits/Catapult.
  - Open-Ended: Build "something," but do not specify materials.
- Time constraint or deadline: The deadline helps students focus on an end goal.
- Focuses on problem-solving: The challenge is in finding a solution to a problem.
- Collaboration: Sometimes we need a buddy to stay motivated.

Design Prompt Tips from the Tinkering Studio

Ryan Jenkins works with a team to prototype space called The Tinkering Studio at the Exploratorium where people can experiment with real tools, materials, and phenomenon. He's involved in planning and leading workshops on tinkering at the museum and around the world for teachers, after-school leaders, and museum professionals.

As Tinkering Studio Education Developer, Jenkins suggests looking for ideas and redesigning prompts from others before attempting to write your own. He explains that a good example of a prompt that has been refined over time when introducing marble walls or marble runs is "to try to make the marble go as slowly as possible."[3] A prompt like this helps people with a start. Jenkins notes that by having participants look at the marble traveling, learners are observing and also trying to change up the normal pattern of the marble. However, this prompt doesn't limit what learners can do after they figure out how to make the marble go more slowly. He suggests starting with something that gets people to slow down, make observations, and come up with different possibilities. After you have designed a good prompt, Jenkins says that facilitators have to work on encouraging makers to explore their own inquisitive ideas and possibilities.

The great thing about starting points like this, according to Jenkins, is that such a prompt starts learners out with a low threshold but does not limit their avenues of exploration. Jenkins discusses the importance of a facilitator as a support for new directions that occur over the course of a workshop. He says that a design prompt should, "opens up investigative explorations." When designing workshops for The Tinkering Studio, Jenkins says, "We sometimes come up with really complex ideas, but we don't want to put all of that out there. We want to see what our makers come up with. Our director Karen Wilkinson maintains that "The big idea is their idea" (Peppler et al. 2016, 161). So we focus on finding ways to keep the workshop focused on learner's investigations (instead of our own investigations). Half-baked workshops come about

---

3. This and all subsequent Ryan Jenkins quotes are from a telephone interview by the author on July 22, 2016.

when you design for the starting points, but not the long-term outcome. In this way, you can have learner's investigations lead the learning.

Tips from Ryan Jenkins of Tinkering Studio When Crafting a Design Prompt

While designing, there are so many possibilities, so think about these:

- What is the best starting point to spark people's interest/curiosity?
- How can we design the starting point to get learners to explore?
- What are the interesting things about this? (e.g., paper circuits)
- How can we make this approachable?
- What are ways to get the workshop focused on learner's investigations?
- Sometimes starting with a limited palette can lead to an open-ended experience.
- Example of a half-baked prototype: "When designing the ScratchX workshop, Jenkins and Catrett created paper circuits examples with a single LED mounted to let learners experiment with programming instead of getting stumped building circuits and then exploring programming."
- "It isn't about making people get an amazing product at the end. It's more about getting people to become curious and wanting to explore concepts further."
- Invite and challenge learners to make the design (and learning) their own!
- Create a closed start that helps learners have a more open-ended experience. ("Start with an already developed block of code and let the learners tinker with that code. Or maybe use an already constructed paper circuit that students can program with an Arduino. The possibilities of what students can do is endless.")
- The "just right" constraint is not too open that you don't know where to start and not so closed or constrained that it only allows for one way to do something (i.e., you end up with no variation or products that are all the same).
- "Try things out with critical friends or colleagues to test out ideas and problem-solve for issues. Make sure your project is approachable and that the process is as important (or more important) than the final product." (Karen Wilkinson, email message to author)

Avoid Competitions

One important element to consider is to avoid making your design challenge into a competition. Maker competitions have always been popular—robotics contests, races, who can make the best/tallest/fastest creation, and so on. The problem with challenges based in competition is that they chip away at the spirit of the Maker Movement. Competitions cause students to be secretive about their designs, to copy others in the hopes of winning, and sometimes even to sabotage other students' projects. Competitions create winners and losers and imply that some students are better than others. This is far from what we want to accomplish in our makerspaces. In contrast, when we take away the competitive element of challenges, students are excited. They want their project to be awesome, and they want their peers' projects to be awesome as well. They're okay with sharing their ideas and talking about their designs. They work in teams and collaborate freely because they aren't worried about whether or not they're going to win. Keep competitions out of your design challenges as much as possible.

Provide a Focus, But Leave Room for Creativity

The limitations and guidelines that you create through a design challenge have the power to give your students focus. Rather than having an infinite number of possibilities in front of them, guidelines help students work on a specific task and a precise problem. If your design challenge is too broad (i.e., make something out of paper), then students might get frustrated with too many options and shut down. However, if your design challenge is too specific and focused (use two sheets of paper to create a bridge that is no more than two inches high and uses a suspension system), then there won't be much room for creativity and variety in what your students create. Aim to find a balance between guidelines and room for creativity.

Build in a Sharing Component

Part of the design process includes communicating your results or sharing your solution. This is a vital part of completing a design challenge as well. Whether students spend hours or weeks on a project, they are proud of what they've created and love to share it with others. In Chapter 2, we talked about connecting your students with other makers through videoconferences and Maker Fests. Consider building a sharing component into your design challenge. Here are some potential sharing components you could use:

- *Have students pitch their project to the group.* This can be pretty entertaining, as students will often reference sales pitches they've seen elsewhere and get quite creative as they advertise their project.
- *Schedule a videoconference.* Whether it's with another school in your district, a maker expert, or someone halfway across the globe, students love sharing their projects through a videoconference.
- *Share student project blog entries.* If you have a blog for your makerspace, have students craft blog posts about their projects and then share the posts via social media.
- *Organize a Maker Fest.* While you probably won't have a full, schoolwide Maker Fest more than once or twice a year, consider holding smaller Maker Fests where students can share projects. In addition, ask students to consider holding on to their projects and sharing them at the larger Maker Fest or at a local Maker Faire.

Crafting a Design Challenge Prompt

Good prompts do not burden a learner, but set them free.
—Sylvia Martinez and Gary Stager, *Invent to Learn*

The wording and presentation of your design challenge prompt can go a long way in ensuring the success of your students. As we mentioned earlier, if the wording is too broad and vague, students won't have focus. In contrast, if you present your students with a detailed 10-step rubric, there will be little room for creativity in their projects. When you craft your design challenge prompt, here are some questions to consider:

What is the goal of the challenge?	What do you want your students to create? What are the final outcomes?
How will you incorporate creative constraints?	By limiting materials? Guiding with a theme? Limiting outcomes? Having an open beginning? Or open middle?
Who can students work with?	Some work might be individual, some in pairs, and some in groups. This can absolutely be flexible. Flexibility in grouping is ideal because that can accommodate the most learning styles.
What materials may be used?	Are students allowed to use anything in the makerspace, or is there a specific material they need to use? Can they bring materials from home? Is there a certain quantity they're allowed to use?
What is the time frame of the challenge?	Design challenges can last for one class period, for entire semesters, and everything in between. But have an endpoint set in the beginning to give more structure. You can always change it later if that's what's best for your students.
How will the project be shared?	Will students be presenting to the class? Sharing in a videoconference? Blogging?
Are there any other guidelines or restrictions?	If there's anything else specific to your challenge, include it at the beginning.

To see these questions in action, let's take a look at a design challenge that Diana has used in workshops with educators:

Using the materials at your table, work with the members of your table to build a tripod to hold a phone or tablet steady while taking a picture. Have one member document your work on a design process worksheet, and be prepared to have one or more members pitch your project to the group. You have 20 minutes.

Now we can break down the statement:

Goal	Build a tripod that can hold a phone or tablet steady
Who	Members of your table
Materials	Materials provided at table (usually K'nex or LEGOs)
Time Frame	20 minutes
Sharing	Pitch to the rest of the group
Other guidelines	One member records a design process worksheet

The prompt is only made up of three sentences, but with those sentences, the educators in the room can clearly understand what they will be doing. This may seem like a simple prompt, or it may seem like every group will come up with the same idea. But over the multiple times that Diana has used this prompt in workshops, she has seen everything from basic, minimalist designs to a working selfie stick to a tripod that can accommodate multiple devices at once. No two designs have ever been exactly alike, and the teachers are quickly engaged because almost all of them have familiarity with taking pictures with their phones or tablets (Figure 5.2 A–D).

Facilitating Student Learning in a Design Challenge

It is important to consider how much involvement to have with students during a design challenge. The goal is to facilitate student-learning experiences without getting so involved that you end up doing the project for them. Think more guiding questions as opposed to telling a student what to do. It's tempting to give kids all the answers and directions and walk them through everything. Yet they learn so much more when they struggle a bit to figure out how to make things work. This struggle is what teaches students how to persevere and problem-solve.

With some challenges, a little basic instruction at the beginning might be appropriate, but do your best to limit this. With the previously mentioned K'nex tripod challenge, Diana will often demonstrate the basics of building with K'nex by showing how some of the pieces snap together.

CROWDSOURCED RESEARCH

Reading isn't about reading. It's about discovery.
—John Spencer and A. J. Juliani, *LAUNCH*

While traditional school library research focuses on databases and online encyclopedias, design challenges and maker projects require answers from experts and resources outside of the traditional canon. Teaching various research models, methods, and skills over the years as school librarians resulted in the realization that the skills we have been teaching for research

a.

b.

c.

d.

FIGURE 5.2 A–D Projects made by teachers using the phone tripod prompt. Photos by Diana Rendina.

are highly focused on academic research. Furthermore, often the research students are conducting is only to solve a hypothetical or highly abstract problem. In projects that involve making, creating, and inventing, this abstract research shifts to researching to solve real and concrete problems or challenges.

Because of the individualized nature of maker and invention-focused projects, students are researching not only for information about their subject but also for needed skills for invention and solutions already discovered by others. Sometimes after playing with a potential idea for a project, students use skill-seeking searches to improve inventions or extend their personal skills to the next level. Skill and solution researching forces students to do self-evaluation and source evaluation simultaneously. For example, a student may want to gain the skill or ability to make an acoustic guitar into an electric acoustic guitar to amplify the sound. They might find several videos on how to do it, but many of them require a drill. If they don't have a drill, they have to search for a solution that fits this design limitation. After they find an instructional video that does not require using a drill, they must evaluate their own skills, resources, time, and learning curve. Can they solder wires together? If the answer is no, can they learn how to solder in a reasonable amount of time to complete this project? Are the tools available to them? In addition to evaluating skills and possible solutions, it is of vital importance that they also evaluate the credibility of the person posting the tutorial to ensure the success of their project.

Online Resources

Resources such as YouTube, Vine, Pinterest, and Instructables where content is crowdsourced are sometimes scoffed at by teachers and librarians who only focus on teaching academically focused research. However, attitudes need to change toward crowdsourced materials because even at the university level, the idea of "open access" is gaining popularity.

Fortunately for our students, the maker community has embraced the idea of crowd-sourced resources by uploading countless "how to" and DIY videos at an amazing pace. Not only can students watch DIY videos, but sometimes students are able to contact the primary source via social media. This real-world research is an excellent avenue for librarians to teach students about evaluating sources for authenticity. Searching for new skill sets and exploring how others have solved similar design challenges offers them opportunities to build on proven solutions, as well as practice communication skills, etiquette, and collaboration.

Tips for Evaluating Sources

- Who is posting this video?
- Are they using an alias?
- If we perform a search for their name or alias, what can we find out about them?

- What are their qualifications?
- Do they run a business or work in this profession?
- Can we contact them safely?

As librarians, we can assist them by modeling how to contact the individual that posted the content. By modeling this action, we can teach web safety in an applied manner rather than a series of warnings and lists of what not to do. Instead of seeking to avoid crowdsourced resources, we need to let students practice judging: reasonableness, reliability, and authority. It's not a huge stretch for librarians either; we have been doing this with print and database sources for years. The questions we ask just need to adjust for new types of media.

Crowdsourcing from Peers

Let's think about how people solve problems and challenges in their daily lives. What do they do when their car suddenly makes a whining noise when turning the steering wheel? How do they avoid paying a diagnosis fee and keep from getting taken advantage of? Most people don't go immediately to a database; instead, they crowdsource by calling their friends who have some skill or experience in working on cars. In other instances, they create a Facebook or YouTube post and maybe include a recording of the sound. Shortly, friends and acquaintances provide a clue to go on that provides accurate terms for searching Google or posting in a forum. If they can't provide a clue, perhaps they supply a name of a trustworthy mechanic. So begins their journey into crowdsourcing to discover why something does or doesn't work.

Inclusive Strategies for Crowdsourcing

- Ask the online community (browse community resources, e.g., Instructables or Facebook group).
- In the classroom, create an expertise survey so students can call on one another for help.
- Use social media to ask the larger maker community for help.
- Check with the local community by calling friends, parents, and local businesses.
- Get help from third-party community experts via services such as Nepris or Skype Classroom.

In the real world, people opt immediately to crowdsourcing and primary sources. Often, these resources are the last ones considered when teaching and planning research because they are viewed as difficult or prohibitive due to the content or subject. The prospect of contacting an expert can seem overwhelming with traditional research projects. However, with Skype, Twitter, and Google Hangouts, this is rapidly changing. Sending a tweet or a message to a scientist, author, or museum expert should be encouraged. Remember to be respectful of the experts' time and also consider this an opportunity to model the potential and positive use of social media.

In makerspaces, we often see students crowdsourcing by surveying their peer groups, whether those groups are assigned or natural occurring. Quick, informal skill and knowledge checks help students get idea of who is an expert. In group work, this provides them with a synopsis of prior knowledge and skills they collectively possess, before moving forward on a challenge. Just like our broken car example earlier, crowdsourcing for skills and expertise can provide direction, a spark for an initial idea, or a connection with an expert guide. It may also mean they may need to keep crowdsourcing to connect with someone who has a skill set or has confronted the same challenge.

Evaluating Resources

Why is teaching self-evaluation and source evaluation to young makers essential when they are viewing DIY videos and other crowdsourced resources? If you have ever decided to fix something at home using a DIY video or copy another maker's design, you likely have made a series of evaluations:

- Do you have the desire to learn and apply this skill?
- Do you have the specialized tools?
- Will you need help or an expert guide?
- Is it cost effective or should this task be outsourced to another person or expert?

While viewing, you probably made some source evaluations without even realizing it:

- Is this person an expert or professional? (dress, affiliations, profile information)
- What do the comments on this video say about the quality?
- Has the owner made other contributions to other resources?

The ability to perform self-evaluation and validate and find credible sources though crowdsourcing is important for all members of the workforce from handymen to medical doctors. Think about a general handyman who has a vast library of DIY videos and Instructables on hand. With smartphones, that library is available to them almost anywhere. If they have the skills to evaluate the validity of those videos and judge whether or not they can make those repairs and look at possible fixes, they become a much more versatile employee. The same goes for doctors, who will need to be able to effectively crowdsource and chat with peers for answers to unidentified problems. Doctors need the research skills that allow them to perform an image search, browse message boards, and quickly communicate with other medical professionals beyond their facility.

It is essential for librarians to teach students how to use databases and books to locate information. In a catapult challenge, students will find it very helpful to browse historical examples of catapults and trebuchets, which are easily located in print. From there, students will feel comfortable moving on to finding more information in databases. Lastly, students can gather championship designs and failures on YouTube before attempting their own iteration of a catapult design. It's important to talk with students about combining both traditional research and new research methods and discuss when it is appropriate to utilize each type.

Action Steps

- Get to know more about design challenges and design thinking (see suggested resources in the Bibliography listing for this chapter).
- Start crafting a design challenge prompt.
- Incorporate crowdsourcing into your next research project.
- Reach out to an expert via Twitter, and model the potential of social media.
- Use Skype or Google Hangouts to chat with experts.

REFERENCES

Fontichiaro, Kristin. 2015. *Design Thinking.* Ann Arbor, MI: Cherry Lake Publishing.

Graves, Colleen. "Starting a School Makerspace from Scratch." *Edutopia* (blog). July 16, 2015. http://www.edutopia.org/blog/starting-school-makerspace-from-scratch-colleen-graves.

Kleon, Austin. 2012. *Steal Like an Artist: 10 Things Nobody Told You about Being Creative.* New York: Workman.

Martinez, Sylvia Libow, and Gary Stager. 2013. *Invent to Learn: Making, Tinkering, and Engineering in the Classroom.* Torrance, CA: Constructing Modern Knowledge Press.

Peppler, Kylie A., Erica Halverson, and Yasmin B. Kafai. 2016. *Makeology. Volume 2.* London: Routledge.

Resnick, M., B. Myers, K. Nakakoji, B. Shneiderman, R. Pausch, T. Selker, and M. Eisenberg. 2005. *Design Principles for Tools to Support Creative Thinking.* National Science Foundation Workshop on Creativity Support Tools. Washington, D.C.

Science Buddies. "The Engineering Design Process." *Science Buddies.* Accessed September 11, 2016. http://www.sciencebuddies.org/engineering-design-process/engineering-design-process-steps.shtml#theengineeringdesignprocess.

Spencer, John, and A. J. Juliani. 2016. *LAUNCH: Using Design Thinking to Boost Creativity and Bring out the Maker in Every Student.* San Diego, CA: Dave Burgess Consulting.

BIBLIOGRAPHY

Cantwell, Mary. "DEEP Design Thinking." 2016. http://deepdesignthinking.com.

D.school. "Bootcamp Bootleg." 2011. http://dschool.stanford.edu/wp-content /uploads/2011/03/BootcampBootleg2010v2SLIM.pdf.

IDEO. "Design Thinking for Libraries." 2014. http://designthinkingforlibraries.com.

IDEO and Riverdale. "Design Thinking for Educators." 2012. http://www.design thinkingforeducators.com.

I2i Experience. "The Innovator's Compass." 2016. http://innovatorscompass.org.

Rendina, Diana. "Teaching the Design Process in Makerspaces." *Renovated Learning.* February 8, 2016. http://renovatedlearning.com/2016/02/08/teaching -the-design-process.

6

Design Challenges with Curriculum Ties for Elementary

If teachers and administrators are having trouble seeing how a school maker-space fits in with the goals of the school, providing curriculum support can be a great advocacy tool. There are many ways to build curriculum connections into makerspace programming. The idea of connecting teachers with resources is one of the best ways for a librarian to facilitate collaboration. However, instead of just providing resources, makerspace activities allow students the opportunities to connect learning concepts to real-world applications.

In the previous chapter, we outlined methods for creating design challenges. When creating curriculum-focused challenges for elementary-aged students, you also need to take into account the considerable age gap in designing challenges for younger students. Plus, think about whether or not you can institute design challenges on a fixed or a flexible schedule.

ABOUT THE EDUCATORS

Because all three authors of this book work in secondary environments, this chapter includes stories from several elementary makerspace experts.[1] Also included in this chapter will be several examples of elementary-level design challenges with curriculum ties.

---

1. Unless otherwise cited, quotes in this chapter are from phone interviews by the author with Andy Plemmons (June 17, 2016), Krissy Venosdale (August 5, 2016), and Todd Burleson (September 17, 2016).

Andy Plemmons

Andy Plemmons is the library media specialist at Barrow Elementary, located in Athens, Georgia. The school has about 600 students and a variety of socio-economic statuses, including students from diverse backgrounds who live in the housing for graduate students from the University of Georgia. Plemmons focuses on creating a participatory culture in his library and constantly partners with teachers from all subject areas. In 2014, his library received a 3D printer, which was the start of his makerspace. Plemmons has transformed the library into a place where students create content rather than consume it (Okyle 2014).

Krissy Venosdale

Krissy Venosdale is an educator with a giant passion for space and STEAM education. She is the Innovation Coordinator at Kincaid School in Houston, Texas. She recently started a makerspace at Kincaid School in 2015. Venosdale began creating the space by taking out a computer lab and replacing it with flexible furniture and shelving for storage with the idea of launching prototypes and ideas. The space was appropriately dubbed the Launchpad, and it is one of many spaces in her school for making. Her students visit her once a week, but she also travels to classes with tools for making.

Todd Burleson

Todd Burleson is a veteran educator with more than 20 years of experience teaching everything from kindergarten to the university level. For the past seven years, he has been the Resource Center Director at the Hubbard Woods Elementary School in Winnetka, Illinois. In 2015, Burleson submitted a proposal to transform his library space with a focus on project-based learning. He was awarded $50,000 and completely redesigned his space into the IDEA Lab. His space now includes a makerspace, video production room, and a giant LEGO and whiteboard hallway (Lynch 2016).

DESIGN CHALLENGES AND TINKERING AT THE ELEMENTARY LEVEL

Plemmons defines design challenges in his elementary school "as open ended tinkering and inventing where you are creating something new, that either solves an authentic problem or answers maybe a specific question that you or students might pose." He doesn't exclusively use design challenges at his school; they are just one part of what he does in his makerspace. Plemmons explains that "a design challenge gives you a tangible objective beyond just tinkering. There is something you are working towards."

It is important to note that Plemmons talks about tinkering with his students a lot. Initially, they didn't understand what the word meant, but now his students know that tinkering is about "pressing all the buttons, trying everything we can try, but we are figuring out how things work along the way. It's not mindless playing; there is a purpose to it." Another key difference for Plemmons is the amount of instructions and specifics given. For example, with younger students, the focus may just be on learning a specific tool to solve a design challenge. Plemmons explains:

> With a kindergartner, I might say 'you are going to use a Blokify to design a new symbol for Winter' . . . whereas the older students I might give them the problem: 'How can we improve lost and found at school?' . . . and they come up with something in makerspace to draw attention to the lost and found.

For Burleson, a design challenge is something that requires the students to work through a process in order to develop a solution. Burleson prefers authentic design challenges over "cute" projects. Tinkering, design, and problem-solving must be realistic and applicable to students. Even "premade" challenges such as using dozens of craft sticks and Dixie cups need to have a purposeful element. Burleson asks students to imagine a real-life problem they might be able to relate it to. For example, his students were having a lot of trouble getting Rigamajig pieces back into the provided wooden cart. He decided to take matters into the hands of the students and let them attempt to solve this real problem. Students brainstormed tons of possible solutions and are presenting their favorite ideas to Cas Hollman, the creator of Rigamajig, via Skype. After presenting their ideas and getting feedback, the students will then go on to develop a storage solution that meets the unique needs of their own learning space.

To adapt her challenges for her younger students, Venosdale likes to focus on "imagination or something they have a strong or direct experience with." There is such a vast gap in what a kindergarten and a fifth grader can do. Older students have more experiences to draw on so making connections come easier to them.

Incorporating Picture Books

Connecting projects with a story is a great way to engage students in making. Maker projects can connect beautifully with literacy. Educators are often tasked with connecting the maker projects they create to curriculum goals. By using picture books as part of a design challenge, elementary educators can easily incorporate making into their lessons.

In recent years, there has been an explosion of excellent picture books with strong ties to making, STEAM, and creativity. Although the following table is by no means exhaustive, the intent is to give educators a starting point for finding picture books and creating design challenges to go along with them. For a picture book lesson, start with a story time where you read the book together as a class. Discuss what you learned from the book, and then dive into your design challenge. Make sure to include a sharing component at the end to spend some time discussing what you learned from the experience.

Book Citation	Suggested Design Challenge
Beaty, Andrea, and David Roberts. *Iggy Peck, Architect*. New York: Abrams Books for Young Readers, 2007.	Using a variety of LEGOs, have students work in groups to create a bridge that can help their mini figures cross a river.
Daywalt, Drew, and Oliver Jeffers. *The Day the Crayons Quit*. New York: Philomel Books, 2013.	Have students work together to design a new home for a box of crayons using a variety of materials. They can use their own crayons to test their prototype.
Spires, Ashley. *The Most Magnificent Thing*. Toronto, Ontario: Kids Can Press, 2014.	Using a variety of recycled materials (paper tubes, cardboard, bottle caps, etc.), have students create their own "Most Magnificent Thing." Have each group write up a story or create a video about what makes their creation magnificent.
Tullet, Hervé. *Mix It Up!* San Francisco: Handprint Books, an Imprint of Chronicle Books, 2014.	Using washable acrylic paint, have student experiment with unusual materials to create paintings. Don't allow paintbrushes. Consider things such as potato stamps, cheap hairbrushes, toys, and other unusual objects. At the end of the lesson, have each group talk about their creation and share why they chose the objects they used.
Barnett, Mac, and Jon Klassen. *Extra Yarn*. New York: Balzer & Bray, 2012.	Teach students the basics of finger knitting (or watch a YouTube tutorial). Using finger knitting or another technique, ask students to create a hat to keep one of their toys warm.
Reynolds, Peter, and Paul Reynolds. *Going Places*. New York: Atheneum Books for Young Readers, 2014.	Give each student or group of students the exact same set of LEGOs (could be a kit or just bags with the same pieces in them). Challenge them to make something unique. Have every-one share their creations and talk about how people can get many different ideas from the same materials.
Breen, Steve. *Violet the Pilot*. New York: Dial Books for Young Readers, 2008.	Using K'nex, have students design their own flying machines. Have the students share how they came up with the idea and how their flying machine would work.
Yamada, Kobi, and Mae Besom. *What Do You Do with an Idea?* Seattle, WA: Compendium Kids, 2013.	Have students talk in small groups about an amazing idea they had that no one else believed could work. Using any materials available, have students design a prototype that represents their idea. When the designs are done, have each group pitch their idea to the class.

K–2 Curriculum Connections

Venosdale shares a common thread with many early adapter maker educators. "I think that I always taught with design thinking, just not formally. I didn't have a name for it. When I discovered making I found my people, my tribe." She was trained in project-based learning and used that training in her fourth-grade classroom. Design challenges involve asking students to solve a problem, but it may not be connected to an empathy piece. Sometimes, Venosdale successfully marries the two. One of her favorite projects to start with younger students is to have them design solutions to solve problems for book characters.

Around Saint Patrick's Day, Venosdale challenged students to design a leprechaun trap:

> We do a lot with imagination because our kids are little. Getting a kindergartner to connect and think about a person's experience is one thing, but getting them to connect with a book character and think about that character's experience is a really easy thing to do. It's innate for them to imagine and think about the princess' experience climbing the tower.

In Venosdale's Launch Pad, challenges can often evolve into design thinking. Some of her students began to think about what would happen after the leprechaun was trapped. "'I'm going to make the leprechaun a TV and bed, so he will have something to do once he's trapped.' Students were thinking about being kind to him," Venosdale said.

Plemmons is also brilliant at connecting curriculum and makerspaces with the classroom. He shared about a class that was doing some project-based learning on space:

> They had an interest in space and had stumbled onto some information about how people were wanting to go to Mars several years down the road . . . they started doing a lot of research about that and wondering how they as kindergarteners could design things to help people with the exploration of Mars. As a class they came and looked at the tools in the makerspace with that question in mind.

The students looked at the littleBits space kit, and explored the possibility of creating rovers with Sphero. They started to explore 3D printing and how they could get food into space. Plemmons used Twitter to engage in conversation with the makers of Foodini, a 3D food printer. Even though kindergartners may be just exploring and not creating a physical object, the ideas they are creating and the research sparked by exploring the tools in the makerspace are equally important.

Plemmons has also collaborated with kindergarten teachers to help teach narrative writing. Students designed their own sculptures and buildings in Blokify on the iPad. "They used that tangible object to imagine going inside and that became the setting for their story." They wrote narrative pieces in their writing workshop based on the designs they created in Blockify.

Working with the art teacher is also a natural fit for making. Part of the curriculum Plemmons's art teacher has to cover is how artists use a variety of tools and technology to create artworks, and 3D printing and modeling make a great fit. The design challenge was to create a pendant. The only requirement was that the pendant had to have a way to connect to a larger piece of jewelry. Students then used Blockify to design pendants because it is a great design tool for students at this age.

A regular design challenge for the second graders is the Barrow Peace Prize. Plemmons explains that "it's a huge project that involves lots of different themes not just makerspace, but it naturally evolved when a student asked the question, 'Why don't we have an actual prize?" Initially, he used Tinkercad to create the prize, but the next year, he had a group of students working to design the prize.

In 2015, Burleson worked on a coordinated study of Jackson Pollock with his art teacher. They incorporated literacy by reading *Action Jackson* by Jan Greenberg and Sandra Jordan in the IDEA Lab. In the art room, students studied Jackson Pollock's techniques and learned more about his biography. Students and teachers alike decided that if Jackson Pollock were alive, he would have been pushing the boundaries of art like he was 50 years ago. He might even use robots to help him make art. So, Burleson and the art teacher brought Sphero robots to the IDEA Lab to create an art piece. After framing a very large canvas with 2×4s, he splattered paint onto the surface of the canvas. Then the students drove the Sphero robots through the paint on the canvas. Each class added a new color, and, in the end, a beautiful collaborative art piece was constructed. The students are all very proud of the magnificent painting that now hangs in the library.

Favorite Design Challenge for K–2 Based on a Challenge by Krissy Venosdale	
Goal	Read *Rosie the Hen*. After reading the book, state that Rosie seems to have a problem finding her way around. Can you design something to help her?
Who	Small-group activity K–2
Materials	Copies of *Rosie the Hen*, cardboard boxes, construction paper, tape, markers, pencils, Duplo blocks, glue
Time Frame	45 minutes
Sharing	Show how your design could help Rosie. Act out how!

Favorite Design Challenge for K–2 Based on a Challenge by Todd Burleson	
Goal	Create a robot sculpture using a variety of wooden geometric shapes.
Who	Members of your table
Materials	Cubes, spheres, hemispheres, a multitude of various wooden shapes and miscellaneous hardware, hot glue gun, and paint
Time Frame	One hour
Sharing	Present your robot to the rest of the class.
Other guidelines (Collaboration?)	Students will come up with a rough design sketch incorporating at least three different geometric shapes. Students will name their robot and develop a name and backstory about their robot.

3–5 Curriculum Connections

Plemmons's third-graders study rocks and minerals and wanted to learn more about design and application, so the students Skyped with a local jewelry studio. They were walked through all the design steps to create a piece of jewelry. After the virtual tour, the third-graders used SketchUp to design and create their own cuts of gems. "They were the first things we ever printed on our 3D printer, and that's when we learned that some designs worked and some of them didn't." To extend the activity the next school year, students discussed ideas for building a climbing wall. Using their learning about the rocks and minerals, they applied their new knowledge of the Mohs Hardness Scale and justified why they would use particular rocks or minerals in their climbing wall design. Students printed prototypes of their final models of their walls.

Another collaboration involved adding some science standards to an ongoing pop-up art project. His fourth-grade team was curious about what they could do with electricity and light connected to their standards. The students were already working on a pop-up book art project. With the addition of an LED and simple circuit, they created a collaboration that achieved this goal.

"I love doing things with the art teachers because they can work on the project in art as well." Students were studying Native Americans in Social Studies, learning about Native American folklore, and looking at dream catchers. Plemmons and the art teacher thought this would be a great opportunity to have students design their own symbol that represented their hopes and dreams for the school year. Using Cubify on the iPad, students were able to turn a line drawing of their symbol into a 3D stamp. Back in the art classroom, they created vessels to hold those hopes and dreams and decorated the vessels with their 3D printed stamp.

Inclusive Strategies

Use a maker collaboration as an opportunity for students to learn about another culture. Have them study the food, art, and society of the culture. Give them opportunities to interview someone from that culture, either in person or through videoconferencing. Have students create a project inspired by what they've learned about that culture. This experience helps students to build empathy as they learn about cultures that are different from their own.

One of the fifth-grade projects that really stood out for Plemmons was a part of larger project called Bookapalooza, where kids created projects around a book they read. Some students did stop-motion retellings of books they read with paper or LEGOs. Plemmons also had students that designed characters from stories they had read. Others built objects out of LEGOs related to the books they read.

When asked how to get to that level of curriculum connection, Plemmons suggests, "It takes a lot of pushing to make these connections happen.

Sometimes I collaborate with whole grade levels, and then sometimes it's a class, or sometimes just a gifted class." The important thing to remember is to work with the teachers that are willing to try something. After one teacher enjoys a collaboration, Plemmons finds that often other teachers will say, "Now that I see what that project looks like, I want to try it too!"

Plemmons also hosts teacher makerspace exploration sessions after school to have teachers experience some of the same things that the kids experience in his library makerspace. With the teachers, he makes a point to ask them to think about curricular connections. The first time he held an exploration, his teachers spent a lot of time playing. Thus, more than just one opportunity is needed to get teachers thinking about how making and design challenges could fit into their curriculum.

Sample Design Challenges

Design Challenge for Grades 3–5 Based on a Challenge by Krissy Venosdale

Goal	Get a marble across the floor without it touching the floor.
Who	Groups of 3–4
Materials	Cardboard, cardboard tubes, scissors, paper, tape
Time Frame	45 minutes
Sharing	Make a quick video.
Other guidelines (Collaboration?)	One member records a plan for each group. Stop and share the successes and failures of plans after 20 minutes.

Design Challenge for Grades 3–5 Based on a Challenge by Todd Burleson

Goal	Create a radial symmetrical design on your quadrant of a LEGO base plate.
Who	Members of a table (grouped into four)
Materials	LEGOs, baseplate
Time Frame	One hour
Sharing	Tables will share their radial symmetry projects
Other guidelines (Collaboration?)	Each student will create a geometric design on their quadrant. Students will then pass it clockwise around the table. The "receiving" student will mirror the creation of the first quadrant. Each successive student will work to re-create the design; the finished product will be a radially symmetrical LEGO design.

Design Challenge for Grades 4–6 Based on a Challenge by Krissy Venosdale

Goal	Design a package to mail an egg.
Who	Members of your table
Materials	Origami paper, straws, tape, cardboard
Time Frame	20 minutes
Sharing	Test the package.
Other guidelines (Collaboration?)	One member records a design process worksheet.

Tallest Structure Design Challenge by Todd Burleson

Goal	Build the tallest structure you can with a single cube as its base.
Who	Members of a table (grouped into four)
Materials	30 Dixie cups, 30 tongue depressors
Time Frame	30 minutes
Sharing	Tables will work together to create a structure that rests on a single cube.
Other guidelines (Collaboration?)	The students will work together to develop the tallest structure. Along the way, they will discover the importance of a strong base and the properties of their various building materials.

SCHEDULING

The library schedule at Plemmons's school is completely flexible. However, he has a unique insight into running maker activities in both fixed and flexible schedules because of his work with his art teacher, who does have a fixed schedule. Librarians can be successful with both types of scheduling.

Fixed vs. Flex

For elementary school libraries working on a fixed library schedule, Plemmons had this advice to give: "You can think in terms of how much time you have with each class and think about what are some realistic projects you can get done in that time." A lot of the collaborations Plemmons has done with his art teacher were done in one session. "If you are going to do something over time, you have to think about how you're going to store the work in progress because that is tricky. It can get out of hand so quickly." Consideration and forethought have to be made about a system of storage and what type of project will realistically store well.

With fixed schedules, you'll also need to consider partnerships, as they allow you to be more flexible with time in your library. Many librarians use partnerships with paraprofessionals, family volunteers, and students who need service hours to take care of the daily library operations while the librarians are collaborating, planning, preparing, and researching. An invitation to help during a makerspace activity also opens the door to many who might not consider traditional library volunteer duties. Reach out to any mentoring groups that meet in the library, and be sure to enlist the help of any clubs and their sponsors if their members need service hours. If there is a university nearby, it is a great place to start building partnerships. Plemmons started a partnership with Gretchen Thomas at the University of Georgia as mentioned in Chapter 4.

A flexible library calendar by nature has the immediate benefit of allowing more elasticity with time and the length of time projects take. You can take several days or just an afternoon if needed. "In a flexible schedule, a lot of times with a makerspace project and 3D printing specifically, you have that time of designing, but there is all that time of prepping the files and getting them printed." With a flexible schedule Plemmons can put that on the calendar and prep and print those files. "When you do every art class for third grade, that is 100 files that need to be printed." For someone with a library that has a fixed schedule, this could present a huge challenge.

Venosdale has a fixed schedule for all the classes to come, but she also has time built in so that the lab is open. It works well for her because she is able to see her students each week but has open times that can be scheduled if a project needs more time. Sometimes, having a time limit can work as a constraint and make them more creative, as Venosdale explains:

> A lot of times, we think if we just give kids full freedom, they will be more creative, but the opposite is sometimes true. I think that is what is cool about the design challenge; you hand students the materials, and give them a challenge like 'Make this light up,' which forces them to really get creative and problem-solve. This challenges them in ways they aren't typically challenged in school.

Burleson has a fixed library and sees students twice a week in the library. Once a week, they have a 25-minute book checkout time in which he introduces various authors, library skills, and so on. However, he also has them for a one-hour block later in the week in which students explore a variety of learning tools in the IDEA Lab.

Plemmons also has an open makerspace time every Tuesday and Thursday from 11:00 a.m. to 12:30 p.m. There is not a specific activity or challenge for students every time, but he tries to pair two different activities or ideas for students. He might pair a craft- or art-oriented activity with a technology-oriented activity that complements it. An example of such a pairing is clay modeling or making pipe cleaner animals and also offering to create stop-motion videos with creations as an option. Students can choose to do one option or pair both options. Plemmons notes, "In that open makerspace time we have on

Tuesdays and Thursdays, I use that time to look at what kids are doing. As I see them exploring the different tools, I think about how they connect to what teachers are doing in their classroom."

Makerspace at Recess and Lunch

Many of students choose to visit the makerspace at Plemmons's school during their lunch or recess. Plemmons uses this time to partner with Gretchen Thomas at the University of Georgia. In their first collaboration, Plemmons's students visited the UGA campus and demonstrated Makey Makey and Sphero alongside Thomas's students. This allowed students who were walking to class to participate and join the fun. Later, the students in Thomas's class visited the school and helped host pop-up makerspaces on the playground. Any student at recess was welcome to join in the fun; it helped students to understand what kind of activities go on in the library during makerspace time. The outdoor environment allows for messier projects such as tin foil boats, bubble wands, and marble roller coasters with duct tape and tubing.

Burleson is also working to develop a program that will allow students to visit the makerspace during lunch. He hopes to offer coding/video game design, sewing, robotics, and more. In addition, his library offers after-school classes in which students can sign up for six-week sessions that focus on a variety of classes. His PTO is also hopeful that they can develop weekend programming for his space. The plan is to use adult-supervised former students as "docents" who guide current students through maker activities.

Action Steps

- Start crafting your own design challenges by forming goals and collaboration ideas, figuring out materials, setting a time frame, and thinking about how students will share final design challenges, along with any other necessary guidelines.
- Seek ways to involve the community.
- Talk with teachers about pertinent curriculum connections.
- Connect with maker experts to extend thinking during design challenges.

REFERENCES

Lynch, Grace Hwang. 2016, August 25. "Yes, He Can! Todd Burleson, SLJ's 2016 School Librarian of the Year." *School Library Journal.* http://www.slj.com /2016/08/industry-news/yes-he-can-todd-burleson-sljs-2016-school -librarian-of-the-year/#_.

Okyle, Carly. 2014, September 3. "School Librarian of the Year Finalist Andy Plemmons: Expecting the Miraculous." *School Library Journal.* http://www.slj .com/2014/09/industry-news/andy-plemmons-expecting-the-miraculous.

7

Design Challenges with Curriculum Ties for Secondary

CRAFTING DESIGN CHALLENGES IN SECONDARY

Diana and Colleen's collaborations began in 2014, when their students first participated in a joint virtual design challenge. It started with a Google Hangout where Colleen's students attempted to teach Diana's students how to make bristlebots, and Diana's students presented their inventive cardboard creations for Caine's Arcade and the Global Cardboard Challenge. That first virtual field trip was chaotic and hectic, but it ended with a challenge by a student who wanted everyone to create catapults. From there, students were flung into their first joint-design challenge, and we quickly learned that students loved having a voice in what they were making. Even though students were only challenged to make catapults, they built trebuchets (Figure 7.1), slingshots, a five-armed catapult, and a catapult so big, it had to be wheeled in on a garden trolley. We offered no grade, no extra credit, and no prize. We just asked, "Can you do this?" The students exceeded our expectations and began an amazing design challenge journey. On the day we met to discuss our catapults, Diana's students set forth a new challenge to create game controllers with Makey Makey.

The Makey Makey Challenge really took hold of Colleen's students at Lamar Middle School. Even though she hadn't taught them to create games in Scratch, the students quickly figured out how they could make their own games and came frequently to the library to ask for help if they were struggling. Colleen set out an Inventor's Box full of bricolage for students to create controllers. When the kids got stuck, Colleen tweeted to the inventors of Makey Makey and set up an inspirational chat that forever changed the maker culture at Lamar Middle School. By talking with these mentor experts during the Makey

93

FIGURE 7.1　Trebuchet designed by Stewart Middle Magnet School students.

Makey Challenge, the students were able to ask questions and start "thinking beyond the banana."

Jay, Liam, Todd, Rachel, and Dave are an awesome team and so down to earth that they spoke to the kids on their own terms. Jay Silver spoke to Lamar students about "creative confidence" and inherent awesomeness. The best thing about chatting with these mentor experts is that they suggested key advice applicable for anyone getting started with a new concept or invention—"Just start making—don't think too long and hard, just start making stuff and see what works and what doesn't." This virtual chat helped build a culture of creative problem-solving and innovation at Colleen's middle school.

Design Challenges and Tinkering at the Middle School Level

Design challenges can allow for fantastic tinkering experiences at the middle school level. When used strategically, as discussed in Chapter 5, design challenges have the power to provide creative constraints and guidance for students, enhancing their creativity. While tinkering tends to be a bit more open-ended and unguided, it can still fit in well with design challenges.

Middle school is a transitional age. Students are ready to take on more responsibility and leadership skills. Yet at the same time, it's one of the last chances for them to really be kids. Using their imaginations isn't frowned upon by their peers yet. It's crucial to provide creative tinkering experiences to students at this age. If they get left out, we risk shutting down their creative spirits.

Design challenges in middle school can be used informally. One example could be creating a passive design challenge with signage in the makerspace. Design challenges can be incorporated into classroom lessons just for fun and can even be tied to the classroom curriculum.

At Stewart Middle Magnet School, Diana ran a club called the Stewart Makers that met for an hour and a half after school once a week. Each month, she offered up a new design challenge to her students. Some of the challenges included the following, which we'll discuss later in this chapter:

- Build an arcade game with cardboard.
- Make something that flings something.
- Create a chariot or cart for Sphero.

By using design challenges with this after-school group, Diana was able to provide a focus for them. Students got excited about taking on a challenge, dreaming up their projects, and sharing them with their peers.

For David Saunders, middle-grade librarian at Greenwich Country Day School, the goal of a good design challenge is "to give students a framework for exploring and pushing past assumptions while also providing a framework for taking risks and teaching resilience."[1] Saunders feels that the design process is collaborative in nature and helps develop feedback and collaborative skills. "This opportunity to engage in the design thinking/invention cycle/ engineering process brings students through the stages of thinking through creating a product." For students in the middle grades, engaging in constructive critical feedback for this age group is key. Saunders teaches his students how to continue the conversation by leading them with the sentence prompt, "Yes, and . . ." so as not to shut down the creative process for others.

Saunders says most middle schoolers are experiencing a "development period of burgeoning awareness of people around them and experimenting with what they can say and how they can be. They are trying on different versions of themselves." Opportunities in the makerspace can help students "try on" the role of engineer, artist, and creator. For Saunders, this is of principal interest and provides a unique opportunity for students to pursue their own learning goals. "Design challenges help students find ways to collaborate and work together on things. The focus helps them pursue things that are of interest to them and may not always be tied to curriculum connections." Makerspaces offer the unique opportunity for a student to proclaim "I'm interested in this and I want to see where I can take this." Saunders believes that "giving them

---

1. This and all subsequent David Saunders quotes are from a telephone interview by the author on July 26, 2016.

these opportunities in middle school sets them up for moving into the academic requirements of high school."

Design Challenges and Tinkering at the High School Level

At the high school level, subject areas become increasingly specialized. Standardized testing increases the desire of classroom teachers to teach lessons that only address their curriculum. Design challenges should be a natural fit for the curriculum. Because of the highly specialized subject areas at the high school level, the librarian is essential in promoting design challenges and thinking opportunities. Yet, the librarian may have to rely more on the subject area teacher to make meaningful connections.

For example, Aaron Graves received a 3D printer from DonorsChoose, and one of his geometry teachers, Sherry Dietrich, really wanted to try 3D modeling with her class. Initially, they thought of making a house or an object with a set of requirements. When he showed her the example of a simple gramophone made with a needle and cone one day when she was in the library, Dietrich immediately saw math connections in the design: surface area, rotation, and speed. They decided that the challenge would be to design a 3D printed object to make the simple gramophone play more consistently or at a louder volume without electricity. She added some math objectives that her students needed to meet, such as calculating the volume of the 3D printed figure and calculating the surface area of anything used to create the gramophone.

Dietrich and Graves let their students play with the example for a good portion of time before issuing the design challenge. During instruction, students were only given basic information about how a gramophone worked. Avoiding too much detail pushed the students to research what caused the simple example to make sound. Some immediately looked up gramophones on their phones or laptops to research how they worked and look at examples.

It only took about 45 minutes for the students to master the basics of Tinkercad and start 3D modeling. The classes met every other day, so students had time to think about design ideas. There were a number of designs that concentrated on making the record into a top or creating an object to help the pencil rotate the record consistently. Other students tried to make plastic tips for the cone and a hole for the needle to sit in so the vibration would transfer better. Some immediately tried to make a larger or longer cone, without even worrying about what they would 3D print because they now knew that the size of the cone affected volume.

Each block, these students were engaged and performing more math than the minimum required objectives prescribed in the assignment. Many students had a moment similar to the scene in the *Karate Kid* when the character Daniel discovers that the movements he has unwittingly practiced such as waxing a car and sanding the floor can be applied to karate. These students had spent years practicing abstract concepts math, and now they were able to apply their learning to improve something in the real world and see a concrete connection. The class followed up the activity by writing thank-you letters to DonorsChoose for the filament that was donated, and, in almost every letter, there was mention of how they had got a chance to apply the math concepts they learned!

CURRICULUM CONNECTIONS IN SECONDARY

The best way to make curriculum connections in secondary is to work with teachers and see what content they need the most help covering. Colleen found that one of her freshman English teachers really wanted an authentic research project that would be engaging for students even at the end of the school year. She proposed having students focus on "invention literacy," a concept articulated by Jay Silver as "the ability to read and write human made stuff, from toasters to apps." After examining Silver's (2016) "Invention Literacy" article and experiencing some maker challenges, students had to research and re-create an invention of their choice with recyclables for this project. While this was a heavily focused maker research project, students also covered core information-seeking skill concepts such as researching historical context via databases, crowdsourcing information via YouTube and Instructables, creating citations, and more.

To get more in-depth with curriculum connection ideas, we've interviewed some awesome maker educators and included their insights and tips. In the next section, we will cover design, reuse, and tinkering design with Patrick Benfield, Dan Ryder, and David Saunders[2] who give tips on connecting making to the curriculum in the English Language Arts (ELA) classroom. In addition, Kristina Holzweiss shares how to accommodate and include makers of various skill levels and more.

Patrick Benfield at the d.lab for Making

Patrick Benfield is the creator of STEAM *by* Design, an approach to education that leverages the powerful ideas and tools of the Maker Movement through the use of design methodologies. As the STEAM and Makerspace Director for St. Gabriel's Catholic School in Austin, Texas, he collaborates with PreK–eighth-grade teachers to thoughtfully integrate these concepts with the curriculum, both in the "d.lab for Making" and in classrooms across the campus.

Teaching Design and Reuse

During a semester-long design challenge, Benfield worked with an eighth-grade science and robotics coach to have students design a gravity-powered go-kart similar to a soapbox derby car. Students used a Google Doc to record all of their design steps and brainstorming; they embedded pictures and designs

---

2. Unless otherwise cited, quotes in this chapter are from phone interviews by the author with Patrick Benfield (July 27, 2016), Dan Ryder (July 27, 2016), and David Saunders (July 26, 2016).

throughout the making of this project. Benfield stressed the importance of daily reflection by asking them questions such as "Did you have any challenges?" Because the collaborative groups did not have the same schedule, students would come to the d.lab to work throughout the school day as needed. This made the shared Google Doc even more important because students could pick up where the last student left off.

Midway through the project, Benfield used Nepris to connect students with a NASCAR engineer to get reflective feedback. This critique with a mentor expert provided students with feedback on their prototype and design from a real engineer. Then students incorporated this advice into their Google Doc and grappled with actually incorporating the advice into their next iteration of their prototypes.

After students built and raced gravity-powered go-karts, Benfield took this challenge further by having students repurpose the same pieces from the go-karts and transform them into a trebuchet. This challenge added a lot of interesting problem-solving for the students because they could only build a trebuchet from the pieces they already had.

Design Tinkering

Benfield loves design and tinkering and considers "design tinkering a broader look at design and making together." Students are still learning through play and natural explorations, but they are also incorporating their own thinking and reflection into what they design.

After students tinker with materials, this knowledge can inform how they complete a design challenge. Benfield suggests, "As an educator, consider what experience you want your students to have, and this will help you plan if you want to teach students through design thinking, a design challenge, or open-ended tinkering."

Goal	Design, build, and race a go-kart.
Who	Eighth-grade science
Materials	Wood, wheels or casters, fasteners
Time Frame	Four weeks
Sharing	During prototyping: Nepris session between each team and a NASCAR engineer
	Final race: in front of the entire middle school students/faculty
Other guidelines (Collaboration*)	Can purchase additional parts after initial purchase
	Only parts physically attached to the go-kart can be used for the trebuchet
	Collaboration via Google Docs/drive
	*The teacher that Benfield collaborated on this with had a content/class-specific rubric for grading purposes.

Kristina Holzweiss and Making Curriculum Connections, Buy-In, Accommodation

Kristina Holzweiss is the librarian at Bay Shore Middle School in Long Island, New York, and the recipient of the *School Library Journal*'s 2015 Librarian of the Year award. She offered this advice to librarians new to making and design challenges: "See what is already in place that you can enhance or supplement. For example, if there is already a curriculum night or a science fair, develop ways to incorporate makerspace activities into these already established programs."[3] Her students view making as a natural part of the library. In a recent maker activity, she connected literature, culture, and making. The activity started with students viewing William Kamkwamba's Ted Talk about how he built two windmills, one to irrigate his family's crops and the other to bring electricity to his home. Having dropped out of school because his family could not afford the tuition, William visited his library to learn more about alternative energy. Through his determination and supplies he found in a local junkyard, William helped to save his family from starvation during the drought in Malawi. Holzweiss's students were then able to read Kamkwamba's life story through a class set of books acquired through a DonorsChoose grant. The project culminated in using the inspiration from the Ted Talk and Kamkwamba's book, as well as in applying engineering, math, and science skills, to create their own windmills using K'nex alternative energy STEM kits. Through this series of lessons integrating literacy and STEM, Holzweiss's students came to realize how fortunate they are to live in the United States. They appreciated the resources that they had and the persistence that William displayed to learn and create despite limited access to education and resources.

Some of her favorite design challenges for getting teachers into the makerspace are Rube Goldberg machines and egg drop challenges. These activities allow young makers to apply math and science concepts they have learned in real-world applications. Holzweiss also connects with her community to foster buy-in at the annual "Parent Camp." She collaborates with a technology teacher to explain genius hour (more info at www.geniushour.com) to the parents and introduce new technology such as 3D modeling and printing. "You couldn't imagine how thrilled they were to discover that their children had access to robotics, coding, a green screen, stop animation, a LEGO wall, and K'nex. Seeing the parents enjoy our makerspace as much as their children was such a joy!"

To accommodate for novice makers, she offers more problem-based challenges such as building a bridge to withstand the weight of a book. For expert makers, Holzweiss challenges them to discover problems in the world and develop solutions. Many of the resources in her makerspace are color-coded for easy use. Kits and gadgets such as K'nex, Snap Circuits, and LEGOs offer color-coded directions and easy-to-use instructions. The use of color-coded resources helps her break down communication and learning barriers for students so that all can participate in challenges.

---

3. Kristina Holzweiss quotes from phone interview by the author on July 26, 2016.

Inclusive Strategies

The act of making knows no language barrier. However, our organization and labeling system can potentially discourage our English Language Learner (ELL) students if they can't understand it. When creating labels for your makerspace storage, try to include images as well as text. Not all students will know the word for marker, but they know what one looks like. Use color-coding and other signals to help students understand how the system works as well.

Dan Ryder and Engineering in the ELA Classroom

Design thinking is focused on empathy and humanity at the core.
—Dan Ryder, high school English teacher

Dan Ryder is a high school English teacher who has transformed his problem-based learning projects with a design thinking lens. When his students were using problem-based learning, he noticed there was not a mind-set framework. The format was good for tools, mapping out ideas, and management, but his students were still making "dumpster" projects. He wanted to see an improvement in the quality of his students' thinking. He found the mind-set he'd been missing when he discovered design thinking. The focus on intentionality, meaning, and things that matter were just what his students needed. Ryder stresses, "It is not about the projects. Instead, it's about intentionality and the importance of empathy and need finding."

Getting Students into Design Process

To get students into the habit of making, Ryder has students begin by creating things that might seem trivial, but eventually his students begin creating things that matter. He believes that "creative constraints breed innovation." So he creates these circumstances, and then students have to learn "to deal with the circumstances and still solve the problem." He finds that "design thinking is engaging for students because they look at everything through a design lens and an empathy lens."

How Might We?

Ryder approaches his entire year with problem-solving at its heart, and he has students look at literature to find the problems that surround the characters. Students then use the essential question, "How might we?" to design solutions based on the character's needs. For example, after reading *Romeo and Juliet*, one student made pressure sensors with littleBits to detect when the Capulets and the Montagues are both in the town square at the same time. If both were present, an alarm would transmit to the Prince. Students would reflect and respond via journaling. Ryder found the rationale evidenced in their reflections showed that they deeply understood the text.

Example of Design Thinking Lens with *Romeo and Juliet*

- What are the problems that Romeo and Juliet are facing?
- What other characters speak to you?
- What are their problems?
- After listing problems, design solutions for the character problems.
- Prove these solutions will work with text evidence from the play.

Students designed and created the following based on the driving question, *How might we design something that meets the needs of characters?*:

- Tiny houses for *Mice and Men*
- Communication devices for Boo Radley from *To Kill a Mockingbird*
- Sensors in the streets of Verona that notify Prince Escalus when the Capulets and Montagues gather and begin to feud for *Romeo and Juliet*
- A mirror for Willy Loman that helps him see his own truth for *Death of a Salesman*

Crowdsourced Research: Student Work around Ethnographic Research

In Ryder's AP literature class, he wanted to tackle a project which demonstrated that literature can be used to solve real-world problem. For this, he reframed the driving question to the following: *How might better understanding literature help solve the problems in our communities?* and *How might we understand the problems in our community?* Students then had to brainstorm and discuss their own definitions of school, classrooms, and community. His students would brainstorm and ideate, and then an injustice would show up, and kids would think about how to design solutions within this framework.

His students wanted to have an impact on the school budget but weren't sure what they could do. Ryder suggested finding the big questions in the literature they'd been studying and then turning those questions into polling questions for the community. Three core questions emerged from their reading:

- What are you willing to sacrifice to help another?
- To what extent is your voice being heard by people who need to hear it?
- What do you feel is the greatest barrier to understanding one another?

The students wanted to bring together a physical and digital space to discuss these three core questions because they felt the questions could help with the school budget problem.

Students decided if they could poll the community and get answers to these questions in an abstract view, maybe as a class they could figure out how to apply the answers to the school budget issue.

Before creating the digital space for discussing the core questions, Ryder's students crowdsourced as part of the design process to find out what type of survey would be the most effective way to get real feedback. "First, my students asked people what they would use before creating the survey. Students asked: Would you use a QR code? Would you use a digital survey? What do people want to experience? What will compel them to action? What do we know about our user?" Based on these crowdsourced interviews, the students created a digital survey that gathered great responses, and this helped Ryder's learners have deep and meaningful conversations about real-world issues. He said these conversations "helped kids gain empathy."

Students even examined the ethnographic nature of the responses to their digital survey. They looked at the survey and identified interesting pieces of this ethnographic information (level of schooling, income, gender, etc.).

Crowdsourcing for Fidget Projects

Students also used crowdsourcing and the design process when designing "fidget projects." Ryder wanted his students to create fidget projects as something for other students with anxiety and stress.

His students gathered data by talking to parents, nurses, and others, and then looked at what users might need before experimenting and prototyping solutions. After initial prototypes, the students field-tested fidget projects with classes and put a few prototypes in the front office to see how people would use them.

After gathering the data, they compiled it and brought it back to the classroom to reflect on these experimental exploratory prototypes and then matched their data up with the research. Some of their field tests led to interesting observations they would not have made without sharing with actual users. One student made a top, handed it to a behavior room, and immediately was told, "no, it is too sharp and could be a weapon." So another iteration was created. Students learned "that if a core user is a teacher who needs to be able to hand the fidget project to a student and that teacher doesn't feel safe, then no matter how well designed the student felt it was, usability wise, it is a poor design." This crowdsourcing effort made students realize that they needed to ask users, "What safety concerns do you have around designing for stress relief?" Students learned the importance of cross-talking research and the discovery of how to do it right.

In the upcoming years, Ryder wants to find a balance between user data and research data. He wants his students to cross-talk with all of the research. "I want to create a moment for this to happen. Let them discover that they need each other."

6–8 CURRICULUM EXAMPLES

Meaningful curricular integration with a school makerspace is essential for building a strong maker culture. When the sixth-grade language arts team was looking to mix things up a bit, they collaborated with David Saunders to build a project that encouraged students to demonstrate their understanding of plot devices through tinkering. With a focus on understanding "turning points" in the narrative arc of a story, students spent time in small groups working to identify that significant moment in their stories. From there, they designed and built interactive scenes, using a combination of materials, to demonstrate their understanding of the concept, as well as their specific interpretation of it for their book. Students then shared their work through a Gallery Walk and displayed their projects in the lobby of the Middle School.

We are including sample design challenges geared toward getting students in grades 6–8 to collaborate on challenges with curriculum connections. Please use these as a guideline and template for your own design challenges, and feel free to change things or adapt them as needed. In addition, remember that many of these challenges can be tweaked to work at the elementary and high school levels as well.

Cardboard City

Cardboard City is a challenge geared toward social studies and math classes. For social studies classes, the curriculum connection is studying the architecture of various areas. Students could be learning about pyramids and landmarks in ancient Egypt or castles of Medieval times. They could be studying landmarks in various states and countries. After studying the architecture of a specific area within the curriculum, initiate the Cardboard City Challenge. Guide students to research examples of architecture and create their own model.

For math classes, look at geometric shapes and designs in architecture. Study how math is used to plan and design buildings. Have students apply what they learn as they build their Cardboard City (Figure 7.2).

Sample Challenge: Cardboard City	
Goal	Build a model of a building using cardboard and other supplies based off of real architecture.
Who	Small groups of students created by the teacher
Materials	Cardboard, hot glue gun, scissors, cardboard cutter, duct tape or packing tape, various arts and crafts supplies
Time Frame	One week (could be longer or shorter if needed)
Sharing	Have students write up a story about their building and who lives there OR have them write about their design process and how they came up with the design. Post the write-ups with the creations, and do a gallery walk around the room so that students can see everyone's designs
Other guidelines (Collaboration?)	Students need to use research to justify their design ideas.

FIGURE 7.2 Cardboard factory designed by a student.

Sphero Chariot Races

Spheros are relatively affordable robots that can really get students engaged. By creating a design challenge focused around one of these robots, students can move beyond the "modern remote control car syndrome" and get creative.

Sample Challenge: Sphero Chariot Race Challenge	
Goal	Design a cart or chariot that Sphero can drive around a race course OR design a modification for Sphero that can allow it to joust another Sphero.
Who	Small groups of students picked by the teacher
Materials	K'nex, LEGOs, and other arts and craft supplies
Time Frame	Three days (could be shorter or longer)
Sharing	At the end of the challenge, have students try out their creations by racing or jousting one another. Make sure to emphasize that it's not about winners or losers.
Other guidelines (Collaboration?)	Make sure to record the races—the videos can be great for promoting your makerspace.

FIGURE 7.3 A student-designed Sphero chariot.

In social studies classes focused on ancient civilizations, spend some time talking about chariot races, jousting, or another form of racing. Watch videos, discuss how they fit in with the culture, and so on. When students are armed with this background knowledge, start the Sphero Chariot Race Challenge (Figure 7.3).

Book Recommendations and Stop Motion
with David Saunders

Peer reviews and recommendations are powerful ways to get books into the hands of our students. Over the years, librarians have used many different ways to highlight the opinions of our young readers. In David Saunders's middle school library classes, he's begun exploring stop-motion animation as a means of building movie trailers for student book recommendations. After deconstructing blockbuster movie trailers, students work in small groups to outline their video and identify the scenes, characters, and settings they want to include.

When planning is finished, they construct and film their stop-motion animations, adding soundtrack and narration along the way. Set up some chairs, draw the shades, pop some popcorn, and host a screening of the trailers during lunch!

Goal	Film a stop-motion animation book trailer.
Who	Small groups of two to three
Materials	iPads, Stop Motion Studio iOS app, LEGOs, cardboard, tape, craft sticks, markers
Time Frame	Two class periods
Sharing	Screen the projects at a class Film Festival during recess, and invite everyone to attend.
Other guidelines (Collaboration?)	Identify a pivotal moment in the plot and demonstrate it visually.

Greek Mythology and littleBits
with David Saunders

After studying Greek mythology, students choose a mythological character and identify the significant object associated with that character.

Goal	Build an object of power for an ancient god, goddess, or hero.
Who	Small groups
Materials	Cardboard, tape, craft sticks, construction paper, markers, LEGOs, littleBits
Time Frame	Two class periods
Sharing	Share via gallery walk or short video highlighting project
Other guidelines (Collaboration?)	After studying Greek mythology, students choose a mythological character and identify the significant object associated with that character.

9–12 CURRICULUM EXAMPLES

Following are some sample design challenges geared toward grades 9–12 with curriculum connections. Use these as a guideline and template for your own design challenges and feel free to change things or adapt them as needed. In addition, remember that many of these challenges can be tweaked to work at the elementary and middle school levels as well.

Sample Challenge: Paper Circuits for Mom	
Goal	Design and create a Mother's Day card with working circuitry.
Who	This challenge is open to all students and is a great lunch or after-school activity.
Materials	Copper tape, LEDs or Chibitronics stickers, markers, cardstock, cr2032 lithium batteries, small binder clips
Time Frame	Two 30-minute sessions
Sharing	Take photos of completed projects and share them on Mother's Day. This is also a great opportunity for students to share what they learned with parents.
Other guidelines	Have plenty of complete examples so students can visualize the circuit. It might also be helpful to use preprinted circuit paths that can be taped under the drawing on the card.

Sample Challenge: Analyzing Makey Makey Poetry	
Goal	Create an interactive poem with Makey Makey, pencil drawings, and Scratch (Figure 7.4).
Who	Individual students
Materials	Paper, pencils, Makey Makey kit per student
Time Frame	One class period
Sharing	Post poetry examples on social media, or reflect on poetry in maker journals.
Other guidelines	Read and analyze a poem, and draw at least four visual representations of the poem. (Or if students are acclimated to exploring materials, have students create exploratory poems with found items and create audio and game play in Scratch.)

FIGURE 7.4   Makey Makey poetry.

Action Steps

- Start crafting your own design challenges by forming goals and collaboration ideas, figuring out materials, setting a time frame, and thinking about how students will share final design challenges, along with any other necessary guidelines.
- Seek ways to involve the community.
- Talk with teachers about pertinent curriculum connections.
- Connect with maker experts to extend thinking during design challenges.

REFERENCE

Silver, Jay. 2016, May 16. "Invention Literacy." *Medium.* https://medium.com/@wakeupsilver/invention-literacy-5915a411e29d#.uzntcnyq8.

8

Crowdsourcing Research and Maker Journals

My makerspace does not take place over my library—it complements it. Most making is inquiry based. There's a lot more research, tinkering, and questioning going on because of the makerspace.
—Gina Seymour, high school maker librarian
and co-director of SLIMEexpo

USING CROWDSOURCED RESEARCH AND MAKER JOURNALS

From Leonardo to Tesla, scientists and artists have kept journals in the form of sketchbooks and lab notes. These journals allow them to keep track of progress, record questions, log failures and successes, and write down ideas. In much the same way, students can use maker journals to record findings and crowdsourced research, outline problem-solving, and sketch ideas. Young makers can record in their journals with a variety of methods, including drawing, sketchnotes, and traditional note-taking. Maker journals help transform traditional research into an authentic learning experience by providing a relevant and practical way to record and document a student's journey and learning process. In the following examples, students will be challenged to make a real impact by problem-solving a need in their community. The examples also show the variety of ways maker journals were used to enhance their learning.

Driving Question

A teacher librarian is an excellent asset for schools as an instructional partner. Colleen was able to work directly with Katherine Myers on a design thinking research project in which students would identify their own problem to solve, crowdsource their research, and work on developing solutions. They would present their solutions and big ideas to community and school members.

For Myers's class, students focused on the big question: *What is a community problem that I can change?* Students brainstormed multiple community issues for the school and town by sketchnoting things they were interested in. They interviewed other students to find out what issues were of utmost importance in the school community. After the interviews, students chose one issue on which to focus their research. To get students thinking, Myers had students sketchnote five things they already knew about the issue. This helped them consider the gaps in their thinking, focus their research, and begin the task of brainstorming solutions.

Crowdsourcing Research

Because design thinking is a human-centered approach, the majority of the research was crowdsourced. For this project, students' research needs varied as much as their unique problems. Teacher librarians need to expand the definition of research and valid sources. While library databases are still pertinent for "scholarly" research, authentic research stresses the importance of teaching students to navigate web sources effectively to locate primary sources. During Myers's research project, students used the web to locate school lunch menus in other districts, conducted phone interviews with other schools and personnel, and even investigated their own cafeteria as a method of research.

One student interviewed others about their opinion of school lunches, then took a personal tour "behinds the scenes" of her school cafeteria. She took her research further and contacted the district director of Child Nutrition Services to discuss better food options for her fellow students. The director was so impressed with the student's crowdsourced research that she asked the student to research healthier food options and get back to her so she could update our district-wide meal plan! This project allowed the students to see that by backing up research with authentic data, they can take what an adult normally considers as a "teenage complaint" to an actual change in their world. When we asked students how they felt about crowdsourcing their research, here are some of their responses:

Student Responses to Crowdsourced Research

"I learned how to make a change in the real world and talk to professional people."

"I learned you can actually do something about a problem if you make an effort."

"We can't change the world, but we can make it a little better by small steps."

"Research is addictive; like a mystery book, you wanna keep digging even when you know it's doomed."

"At first I was reluctant and lazy, but I became more and more passionate about it over time. The lady that came to talk to us really brought up my morale. I learned that I should be more conscious about my world and to be grateful."

"After this project, I realized that there are so many problems around us that we don't have solutions for. If we made solutions for those problems, we could make society better. I learned that fixing a problem is very important.

"I liked this project because it connected classroom learning to problems in the real world."

"I learned how to formulate data I have collected into usable information that could be presented to others to inform them on a certain topic."

To further incorporate design thinking and crowdsourced research, after students identify the problem they want to solve, they can interview other students about the specified problem. Thus, students can learn how the problem affects others and start thinking about how to design a thing or an idea to solve this particular problem.

Prototyping/Maker Journals

Throughout the research project, we had our students keep designs, blueprints, ideas, and research in maker journals. We encouraged them to sketchnote interviews and research, but we did not require it. Many of our students chose to create campaigns as ways to solve the problem. Not all problems require maker designs; many problems can be fixed with ideas and workflow solutions. This is actually a very authentic way for teens to learn about changing something that bothers them in the world.

If students chose to design solutions for their problem, they would use the journal to sketch prototype solutions and reiterations of prototypes. If students are new to keeping maker journals, you'll have to prep them by sharing engineering journals.

Presenting to Experts

Although many teachers might choose to skip this step, sharing student work with adults is empowering. Invite superintendents, community members, teachers, and more to listen to the students' proposals and design solutions. Many times, all you have to do to get people to listen to student work is ask. Almost everyone invited to Myers's classes was overjoyed to come. On the day of the presentations, sit experts at small tables around the library. This way students will only be presenting to a small group of people rather than getting nervous in front of a large group. For Myers's students, it made the presentation more intimate and allowed students to feel comfortable gathering feedback from these incredible adult listeners. As her students presented to the small group, the experts took notes and listened carefully, and then conversed with students about their great ideas and how to take them further.

Next year, Graves and Myers hope to incorporate this small group presentation earlier on in the research process so that students can take research and design solutions further after gathering feedback from the adult experts. Because the students felt so empowered to go further with projects after listening to the adults, this would be a great way to get students taking that small change to a bigger step in solving the community problem. Plus, this type of project teaches students to persevere through real-world problems and bring about an actual change in their own community. Upon reaching the end of the project, ask experts to come back and see how the student ideas grew after gathering feedback. Students will finish this research feeling empowered that they really can change the world we live in!

Reflection

While students are presenting ideas to experts, the rest of the class should spend time reflecting on the whole process. Frame some open-ended questions and have students spend time writing responses in their maker journals.

Examples of Reflection Questions

- What was easy about this project?
- What was challenging?
- How did you feel about this project? Why?
- What did you learn?

Making time for reflection throughout the project will also make students' ideas and solutions grow. If possible, make daily time for reflection throughout the process. In the next section, you'll learn how an engineering teacher, Ana Josephson, had her students take turns blogging as a form of reflection.

OTHER CASE STUDIES

The best way to understand how to use crowdsourcing research and maker journals is to see them in action. In the following section, we have gathered case studies from several maker educators who used these methods. These real-life examples will help to exemplify how three very different techniques can be used in your own collaborations with teachers.

Ana Josephson and Project Ventura

Ana Josephson[1] has taught engineering at the Ann Richards School for Young Women Leaders for six years and is now also a teacherpreneur at Maker Ready. At Ann Richards, she was tasked with two awesome maker-focused classes. One is a project-based Maker Studio class charged with running a Maker Faire, and the other is a survey engineering course, which is the focus for this study. In her Maker Studio class, she teaches students how to make lots of different things the first semester, and then the second semester, the students create activities for others to make during their year-end Maker Faire. Because her classes are largely focused on project-based learning, she finds that one of the most pertinent aspects of a maker-focused project is the element of sharing. For both of these student-led, student-driven classes, Josephson finds that her students feel empowered after sharing their skills, learning, and knowledge with others. She says that these experiences help her students, "grow and feel a sense of pride. It gives the kids something to talk about with adults that is significant and is something that the students are passionate about." These very real experiences in her classes motivate her students to do more than they would in an average project.

Outline of Project Ventura

Students learn that "Life is about giving, it's not all about me."
—Ana Josephson

Four years ago, Ana was living in a small Airstream trailer while she was working on designing her own house on the same lot. As an artist, she realized she needed more space, and she bought an extra trailer to function as a studio but soon discovered it was riddled with problems. Around the same time, school was starting, and she needed to plan for the large "Cornerstone" project that had been robotics based. She'd noticed in teaching her 10th grade engineering students that they needed more hands-on experience in making and improving things on their own. When her students used a drill, they would be giddy with excitement, and she realized that the girls in her engineering class didn't know how to build anything with their own hands. This was before Ann Richards had a makerspace, and Josephson started thinking, "I have this 12 ft trailer sitting on a lot, what if the girls redesign this trailer as an Eco trailer, kick-start

---

1. Information regarding and quotes from Ana Josephson are from a telephone interview by the author on July 7, 2016.

the funding, and use this as their Cornerstone Project?" She pitched the idea to her administration, and they loved it. That first year, the kids formed design teams, wrote design briefs for clients, took measurements, and raised money through a Kickstarter campaign. Google thought that first project was so amazing, the company gave Ann Richards School a $10,000 grant to do it again the next year! During the second year of this project, the students used the design cycle to transform a 1977 Airstream into a teacher's lounge. Impact Austin, a group of women who give grants to local schools, honored Ann Richards with a $100,000 grant for a makerspace. Because of this trailer, the whole maker movement took off at Josephson's school.

For the 2015–2016 school year, Josephson let the students choose the project based on a problem that they wanted to solve. Because Josephson has certain things she needs to teach through her class, she worked collaboratively with the students to come up with an idea. As the school is 6th–12th girls, the high school students "wanted a place of their own," so the girls decided to design a courtyard and outdoor use classroom for juniors and seniors only. They wanted to create a special place for their grade levels to have class, watch movies, and eat lunch.

Design Solutions

In her class, the girls broke into small groups to come up with their own design solutions for creating a special courtyard just for their grade level. Collaboratively, the girls came up with designs, researched, and created prototypes.

Josephson taught students to use SketchUp for prototyping ideas for the larger architectural aspects. Her students would brainstorm ideas of what they wanted their solution to look like, then draw it, and finally incorporate the engineering concepts they've been learning about in class (e.g., research types of wood).

Research and Journals

Her girls worked with the school librarian on research skills such as locating reliable sources, evaluating sources and materials, and designing through research. This was done all while keeping information in their engineering journals. These journals held the students' brainstormed ideas, hand-drawn designs, research about materials, and thoughts about applying engineering concepts to their design ideas (see Figures 8-1 to 8-5).

Vision Boards and Design Matrix

Because real designers use vision boards when coming up with design ideas, Josephson thought this would be an excellent way for the girls to keep track of ideas. Many students saved pictures to a Flickr account, while others used

Pinterest boards to keep track of ideas. The girls printed out pictures for their vision boards, including paint swatches, trinkets, SketchUp Models, design team logos, and mottos, and some even added real small-scale models to their vision board. During the research and design visioning process, the girls stored their vision boards in a space in Josephson's classroom.

When the girls had to present their ideas to the school, they employed the vision boards as a tangible tool to help them explain their personal design process and how their design would address the needs of the client.

Josephson helped the girls focus on the importance of function and self-evaluation. "A great idea is one thing. But creating that idea in the real world, you really have to take into consideration: Can we complete it on time? Do we have the skill set to complete it?" After the girls presented their ideas to the public, they held a session in class to discuss function and self-evaluation. Josephson asked the class, "The public chose this beautiful design, but what can we really do? Can we really complete it on time?"

When asked, "How do we teach students what they cannot do?" Josephson remarked, "Let them discover that themselves. Let them see a failure as a learning experience and realize that when they can't do something, they can find their own way to learn how they can do it. Ask or find someone to teach them, take a class, etc." And, all must be done within balancing risk and safety protocol. (For more on safety standards at Ann Richards, refer to Chapter 4 where Oren Connell discusses his safety procedures.)

Reflection through Blogging

While the girls actively reflected in their engineering/maker journals, Josephson felt it was important for them to share their process on social media through blogging. To keep the blog active, Josephson created a rotating schedule so that every student was responsible for two posts every six weeks. Every day, a student was assigned to write a post based on a rubric that asked the student to reflect on what she was researching at the moment and how she would incorporate that research into the design idea. This focus on literacy and writing gave the girls an authentic reflection tool with an authentic audience. The girls shared the blog with Josephson, and all of the past annual projects are kept on this same blog: Project Ventura (https://projectventura.com)

On their thoughtful posts, the girls discuss a lot of trial and error in their reflections. Josephson equates this to her partnership with Maker Ready and J. E. Johnson. One of the reasons she feels like the kids are learning trial and error is because she is learning alongside them. "This is the key part to teaching students trial and error. I tell my students. The time we did this was the first time I ever did it. I'm learning with you." She goes on to say:

> If I knew how to do everything, then I would be the sage on the stage telling you how to do it. Since I don't know how to do everything, we have to look it up, talk, and just try it. And if it doesn't work, we take it apart and try it again. We go for it. We make prototypes and if they don't work, we do it again. Model making is

important. I am there learning alongside them. We might watch a YouTube video and think we can do it, but then we try and it's hard and we discover a new skill set we need to learn. When you try to do it yourself, you realize it's very hard. It's the best way to learn. It's the type of education you can't get from a book or a website. There is nothing that can compare to you figuring it out yourself. Once you've figured it out yourself, you become the expert.

Expert Panel

Just like in project-based learning, Josephson ended this massive research and engineering design process by having students share with a panel of experts made up of a retired engineer, community members, and people from UTEACH Texas. The girls were scared, but they beamed with pride after they began sharing and presenting their semester of hard work. By talking about the process with experts, the girls realized that they should be proud of themselves and what they've accomplished. Josephson says that "talking about the process should never be left out. Talking and sharing validates the student's learning."

A Look at Josephson's Students' Maker Journals

FIGURE 8.1 Maker journal covers by students. Photo by Ana Josephson.

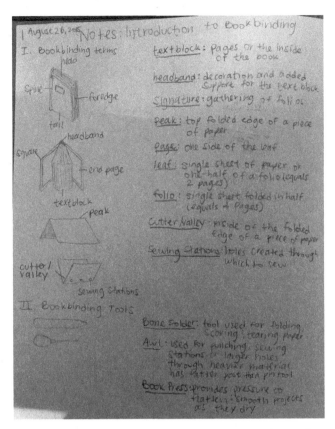

FIGURE 8.2 Maker journal research notes by student.
Photo by Ana Josephson.

Mark Barnett, the Geekbus, and Engineering Design Notebooks

Mark Barnett[2] is a distinguished leader in the area of STEM and maker education and advocates for equity and access to all students. He serves as chief IT strategist at the Intercultural Development Research Association, co-chair at the Libre Learn Lab Conference, and co-chair of the San Antonio Mini Maker Faire, and he has presented at national conferences such as TEDx, SXSWedu, and FabLearn. The Geekbus is a high-tech classroom on wheels that travels to schools, libraries, and other youth-serving organizations to teach students introductory skills in computer science, 3D printing, robotics, video game design, and hardware engineering. The goal of the Geekbus is to provide STEM

2. Information regarding and quotes from Mark Barnett are from a telephone interview by the author on July 19, 2016.

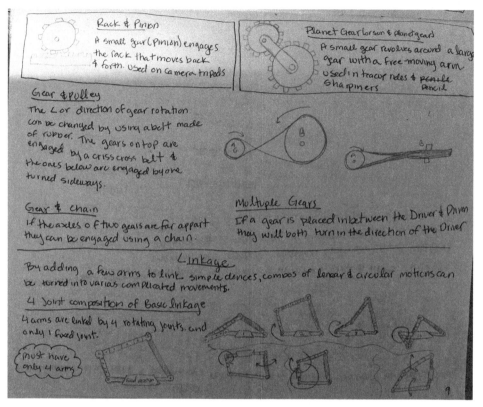

FIGURE 8.3 Maker journal gear notes by student. Photo by Ana Josephson.

enrichment opportunities to underserved youth that may not have access to high-tech learning experiences.

Engineering Notebooks

Mark has been using engineering notebooks for teacher professional development for a few years and uses the same process with students. He uses the very formal *Make: Magazine* blue notebooks that actually have electrical engineering notes in the back cover (Figure 8.6). The important thing about having a notebook is personalizing it. Students can build circuits into it and light up the notebook.

He utilizes notebooks when the Geekbus is hosting a weeklong camp with constant contact with students. He starts out by sharing examples of Tesla and Einstein's notebooks and explains the importance of handwritten and hand-drawn examples when documenting iterations and prototypes. Barnett works with teachers on how to set up notebooks, how to document the design process, and how to create technical drawings. Teachers and students practice technical drawing by making a drawing of an everyday object (e.g., phone, iPad, marker, etc.). Participants use a ruler to document the width, height,

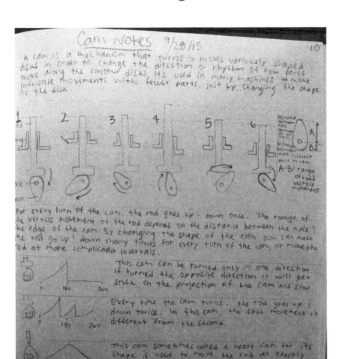

FIGURE 8.4 Maker journal cam notes by student. Photo by Ana Josephson.

and details they want to add. He shares practiced examples of old iPods, teacher examples, and so on (see Figure 8.7).

Teachers cut out and tape the "guidelines for creating engineering notebooks" into their journal. It is much like a science journal or traditional English journal, where all pages should be used, and students should not tear pages out. If they want to add something in, they can tape it into the journal.

Setting Up Notebooks

Students use the notebook as a documentation of their thinking process. It's a reflective piece to write down the problems they encounter and solutions to the problem they find while they are making. They use the notebook to ask questions and reflect on what they learned throughout the project. At the end, they use the Socratic Seminar to crowdsource answers for all projects. Instead of asking the teacher for answers, the whole group problem-solves together to come up with answers for other students.

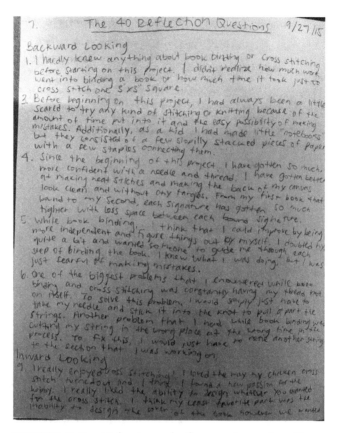

FIGURE 8.5   Maker journal reflections by student. Photo by Ana Josephson.

Barnett stresses the following to students regarding notebooks:

> While you are working, everything is fresh in your mind, but a few months down the road, it will be harder to remember what you did. That is why it is important to write down and document your process because it will be easier to recall later. This is why famous scientists use engineering notebooks, so they can document what they are working on so they can recall it later.

He shares many examples of famous scientists' notebooks because students ask, "What do I document?" See Figure 8.8 for a list of ideas (interviews, sketches, written ideas, sequential information). Barnett frontloads students with the "why" of a notebook by showing lots of examples—both famous and personal. He also shares with students how a well-documented notebook can even be used in legal hearings or testimony. "The only reason why Tesla is credited with some of his inventions is because of how well he documented his ideas in his engineering notebooks." By frontloading the purpose of keeping a notebook and providing historical context, it gives students a purpose in learning how to take accurate notes. This method of teaching note-taking when

FIGURE 8.6 Engineering notebooks by Mark Barnett.

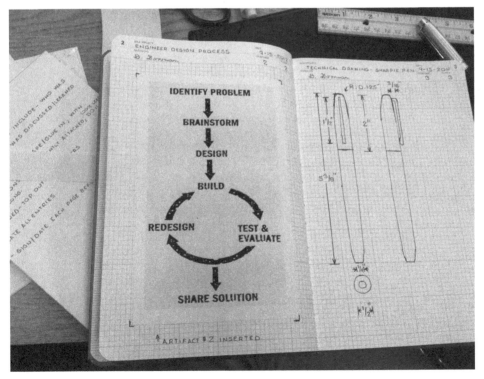

FIGURE 8.7 Technical drawing by Mark Barnett.

habit forming actually "helps students with everyday note-taking because it gives them a purpose for learning this skill."

The notebook itself "becomes an artifact of learning, and students can physically hold in their hand what they learned!" Students must be taught the importance of accurate documentation. Notes should be precise and detailed with logical explanations, drawings, and sketches. Barnett says that modern iterations of this process could include sketchnoting techniques. Students can print photos, cut out, and glue in. He tried digital notebooks, but he found that unless the students are already using an iPad as part of the instructional process, the notebooks may end up not being used to the fullest extent.

Guidelines and Suggestions for Engineering Notebooks:

1. Always record written entries legibly, neatly, and in permanent ink.
2. Never, under any circumstances, remove pages from your notebook.
3. Never let anyone other than yourself write in your notebook (excluding witness signatures).
4. Start entries at the top of the first page, and always make successive, dated entries, working your way to the bottom of the last page.
5. After completing a page, sign it before continuing to the next page.
6. Never leave blank spaces, and never erase or remove material you have added. Simply draw lines through any blank spaces at the same time you are making your entries.
7. Do not erase errors. Just draw a single line through any erroneous entry, and then add your initials. Enter the correct entry nearby.
8. Immediately enter into your notebook and date all original concepts, data, and observations, using separate headings to differentiate each.
9. All information, notes, sketches, designs, and so on should be recorded directly into your notebook. Notes and calculations should be done in your notebook, NOT on loose paper.
10. Label all figures and calculations.
11. To insert pictures or outside information into your notebook, tape the picture into your notebook and outline with permanent ink to note that it was there in case it falls out.
12. Never rely solely on any supplemental attachment. Always include your own entry describing the attachment, and add any conclusions that you might draw from its substance.

Every notebook is a work in progress, forever changing and developing. There is no such thing as a *final* copy of your notebook; the *real thing* is complete with misspellings, stains, worn edges, and wrinkled pages. Just remember to keep it real!

Don't be afraid to customize your engineering notebook to reflect your team's personality! At the end of the training, this notebook will be a great piece of memorabilia from your HSTEAP experience.

FIGURE 8.8   *Engineering notebook handout by Mark Barnett.*

Use in Reflection

There are many aspects to the process of creating soft circuits. So when Barnett's students take this project on, he has them document in their notebooks how to make a circuit. Then they build a circuit out of paper clips and batteries and draw that in their notebook. Students practice stitching, and then they draw and document what a stitch looks like in their notebook. He has students combine these ideas and then think about the following: "Where would you stitch a circuit? Where would the light go? Where will you place the battery?" It is important for them to draw the front side and the back side of the project they will make and include measurements.

Sewing circuits can be quite a complicated process to teach students if they do not have previous experience sewing. Barnett's method of chunking the learning by teaching circuits and sewing separately and having students document their process along the way can be very helpful. It can saturate their learning and ease frustration later on when students are knee deep in making.

Patrick Benfield, Design Tinkering, and Maker Journals

Patrick Benfield[3] loves design and tinkering and considers "design tinkering a broader look at design and making together." Students are still learning through play and natural explorations, but they are also incorporating their own thinking and reflection into what they design.

After students tinker with materials, this knowledge can inform how they complete a design challenge. Benfield suggests, "As an educator, consider what experience you want your students to have, and this will help you plan if you want to teach students through design thinking, a design challenge, or open-ended tinkering."

Pre-K and Maker Journals as a Preemergent Literacy Tool

The St. Gabriel's prekindergarten program is inspired in part by the Reggio Preschool model where students explore and play as their primary mode of learning. To start the year, teachers read and share the book, *How to Be an Explorer of the World: Portable Life Museum* by Keri Smith. This book offers a series of playful, thought-provoking explorations meant to highlight the similarities between scientists and artists. This idea provides a natural starting point for these young students to begin their journey into making.

Because they are barely emergent spellers and writers, Benfield and the pre-K team focused on the book's "field work," that is, playful explorations of everyday things. Benfield says that students are "using these explorations as a way to develop a maker mind-set by treating one's world like a giant, playful science lab that's full of potential discoveries." He finds that it helps these young

---

3. Information regarding and quotes from Patrick Benfield are from a telephone interview by the author on July 27, 2016.

learners nurture their curiosity and sense of wonder by slowing down and noticing the world around them.

Even though the students are not reading and writing yet, they chronicled and reflected on their field work activities in a variety of ways, such as drawing pictures, sharing observations, and working together to analyze, compare, and sort found objects. He wants students to feel comfortable being an artist and a scientist at the same time.

Exploration #1: Have students notice things with words on them, talk with them about typography, take a learning walk around campus, let students look for letters and words they find interesting, and have them draw these letters into their journal.

After Exploration #1, Benfield and collaborating teachers noticed that the pre-K students were not only "seeing things differently, seeing the beauty in unexpected places, but actually practicing letter formation at the same time." Exploring is an excellent way to encourage how the maker mind-set and learning go hand in hand.

Exploration #2: Have students find faces/shapes/and so on in everyday things with the idea that students will explore and then collect objects to make a mini museum.

After Exploration #2, students made collections with their found materials for a tiny mini museum. Benfield had them sort their collections to see how they would combine things. Some students combined by color, and some sorted by manmade objects. Benfield notes that, "It was an interesting exploration that led to teachers seeing how they (the students) were thinking."

His pre-K students went even further with this concept by building tiny museums that would hold their tiny collections. Initially, they drew designs on paper, architecting and designing buildings, and coming up with wildly creative ideas. Because not all of their designs would be possible engineering wise, Benfield asked students, "How can these ideas be made real?"

This helped them transition from designing 2D drawings into 3D objects by exploring and testing materials. Soon his pre-K students were pounding away with a hammer on a stump and learning to use power tools. Plus, Benfield was excited to see that "by the end of all of these explorations, they all came together to make the museum." By combining the physical work with drawing and designing in the journal, students were able to create a tiny museum for their collections. The teachers realized that it was a great way to see that the students' "thinking process can be both drawn and written about, but can also be explored and shared. It was just enough structure blended with creative play. It was very empowering for students because they learned how to use tools, and learned a social element of how to collaborate and help each other out."

Materials Journal with Second-Graders

We do not learn from experience . . . we learn from reflecting on experience.

—John Dewey

At the d.lab second-grade students created "Tinkering journals." Before jumping in, Benfield finds that it is good to work with materials and explore materials because this will lead to deeper thinking. Students focus on exploring materials and questioning, "What is possible with this material?"

Each page of a student's tinkering journal has a sample of each material. Second-graders then experimented with materials to explore the possibilities. By physically exploring materials and taking notes on the engineering properties behind them, students were able to create their own material libraries. In this way, when students wanted to use a material later in a project, they would have an idea of what material would be best for each specific project (i.e., waterproof material, bendable material, etc.).

Material Journal Prompt Examples

- How does it change over time or with force?
- Can you tear it?
- Can you squish it?
- Can you shape it?

This materials library is based on something designers actually do, but Benfield really wanted students to have a portable material library, so they created this in a portable tinkering journal. Not only do students explore the material, but they spend time reflecting on what they can do with the material. Benfield suggests having students reflect by "boiling down the most important aspect of the experience into a one-sentence headline."

Action Steps

- Try incorporating sketchnotes or another form of visual note-taking into your next maker project.
- Add crowdsourcing as an important element of research in your instructional practices.
- Incorporate design thinking and an empathy-based approach into research projects or design challenges.
- Get a book like *How to Be an Explorer of the World: Portable Life Museum* or *The Steal Like an Artist Journal*, and have your students work through one of the prompts.
- Brainstorm ways that maker journals could work as an instructional practice on your campus.

BIBLIOGRAPHY

Cantwell, Mary. DEEPdt. http://deepdesignthinking.com/the-deepdt-learning-means.

Graves, Colleen. "Importance of a School Library Makerspace—in Rural and Low Income Schools: Capitol Hill Maker Faire." June 20, 2016. https://colleengraves.org/2016/06/20/capmakerfaire-advocating-for-library-makerspaces.

Kleon, Austin. 2015. *The Steal like an Artist Journal: A Notebook for Creative Kleptomaniacs*. New York: Workman Publishing Company.

Smith, Keri. 2008. *How to Be an Explorer of the World: Portable Life Museum*. New York: Perigee.

Glossary

Arduino—An open-source physical computing device (microcontroller) and electronics platform that can be programmed in a variety of ways (https://www.arduino.cc).

Badges—Physical or digital tokens that are given out when students complete a particular task or master a particular skill.

Barnett, Mark—Chief IT strategist at the Intercultural Development Research Association, co-chair at the Libre Learn Lab Conference, co-chair of the San Antonio Mini Maker Faire, and presenter at national conferences such as TEDx, SXSWedu, and FabLearn.

BLAST (Building Leadership And Strengths Together)—A class for at-risk teens (similar to AVID).

Blokify—A 3D modeling software app geared toward children (http://blokify.com).

Bricolage—A French word for the construction and creation of things using a variety of diverse materials.

Brushbot—A simple robot made with a motor and a scrub brush.

BYOD (bring your own device)—A school policy that allows students to bring personal, Internet-connected devices to use at school.

Caine's Arcade—A short film by Nirvan Mullick about nine-year-old Caine Munroy, who built an arcade out of cardboard in his father's shop (http://cainesarcade.com). See also Global Cardboard Challenge.

Catapult—A device that throws an object.

Chibitronics—Surface-mounted LEDs on a sticker.

Creative Constraint—A design constraint that makes students think creatively; see more information in chapter 5.

Crowdsourcing—A practice of collecting information or resources from a crowd of people often using online communities.

Cubify—A 3D printer manufacturer, now a part of 3D systems (http://www .3dsystems.com).

Design Challenge—A prompt to focus student designs. Includes goal, time frame, materials. See Chapter 5.

Design Thinking—Empathetic or human-centered design. See Chapter 5.

DIY—Do it yourself.

DonorsChoose—A crowdfunding website for public school educators (https:// www.donorschoose.org).

Dot and Dash—Bluetooth-enabled robots created by Wonder Workshop that can be programmed and coded through a variety of apps (https://www .makewonder.com).

Ethnographic—A study of people in their environment using observation and interviews.

Facebook—Social media website (https://www.facebook.com).

Fixed Schedule—A schedule that has set regular times for class visits to the library.

Flexible Schedule—A schedule with no set times, allowing users to schedule their own time in the library based on need.

Flickr—Photo-sharing social media website (https://www.flickr.com).

Foodini—A 3D printer produced by the Natural Machines company that uses fresh ingredients to create printed edible food.

Geekbus—A high-tech classroom on wheels that travels to schools, libraries, and other youth-serving organizations to teach students introductory skills in computer science, 3D printing, robotics, video game design, and hardware engineering.

Global Cardboard Challenge—An annual event in October where people of all ages build things out of cardboard (http://cardboardchallenge.com). Inspired by the short film, *Caine's Arcade*. See also *Caine's Arcade*.

Global Youth Service Day—An annual event gathering young people in community service (http://www.gysd.org).

GoFundMe—A crowdfunding website that anyone can use (https://www .gofundme.com).

Google Hangouts—A communication platform available online and in app format that allows users to communicate with voice calls, video calls, and instant messaging, and allows users to share attachments.

Hashtag—Used in social media to group posts together or designate a specific association. Starts with the pound sign followed by a word or group of words such as #stewartmakes.

Holzweiss, Kristina—Librarian at Bay Shore Middle School, in Long Island, New York, and the recipient of the *School Library Journal*'s 2015 Librarian of the Year award.

Ideate/ideating—Forming ideas or concepts.

If-then statement—A conditional statement in coding and mathematics.

Instructables—A website for sharing, creating, and viewing tutorials on a myriad of subjects (http://www.instructables.com).

Invention literacy—Understanding how things work so that makers can re-create and create new things.

Iteration—To repeat a process or create a revision of a design.

Jenkins, Ryan—Education developer at the Tinkering Studio.

Josephson, Ana—Former engineering teacher at the Ann Richards School for Young Women Leaders for six years; now a teacherpreneur at Maker Ready.

K'nex—Engineering toys that snap together in a variety of ways (http://www.knex.com/knex-education).

Laser cutter—A tool that uses a laser guided by computer numerical control (CNC) to cut materials such as metal, leather, or wood.

LED—Light Emitting Diode.

LEGOs—Plastic building blocks that snap together (https://education.lego.com).

littleBits—Electronic building blocks that attach magnetically to create inventions (http://littlebits.cc).

Make Magazine—A bimonthly magazine focused on DIY projects and culture; first published in 2005 (http://makermedia.com/brands/make-magazine).

Maker—Someone who finds joy in making things, whether physical or digital.

Maker Faire©—An event that celebrates making and DIY culture. Started in 2006, they are now held throughout the year around the globe.

Maker journals—Journals used to record the design process of makers. See Chapter 8.

The Maker Movement—A global movement focused on DIY culture.

Makerspace—A place where visitors can explore and create both digitally and physically using a variety of tools and resources. Makerspaces can be public, nonprofit, in school, library, and so on. See also Chapter 1.

Makey—The logo for *Make Magazine* and the magazine's robot mascot.

Makey Makey—A plug-and-play device that can be used with any USB compatible computer or device. It can turn any conductive material into a computer key (http://makeymakey.com).

Marble wall—A wall with tracks or obstacles for marbles.

Miter saw—A saw that uses a guide to make accurate cross and angled cuts.

MOOC—Massive Open Online Course. A free online course that anyone can participate in.

Nepris—A cloud-based platform that allows educators to connect their students with industry experts.

1:1—The education method where the school or district provides at least one device per student. Usually this is a device that students can take home with them, but it remains the property of the district.

Paper circuits—Electronic circuits made using batteries, copper tape, and LEDs.

Pinterest—A social media site for sharing resources and websites using graphical images from the resources called "pins." Users can create boards for various topics (https://www.pinterest.com).

Pollock, Jackson—An American abstract expressionist painter known for his drip painting style.

Project-based learning—The Buck Institute for Education defines project-based learning as a teaching method in which students gain knowledge and skills by working for an extended period of time to investigate and respond to an authentic, engaging, and complex question, problem, or challenge.

Prototype—A rough draft of an invention or a project.

Qualitative—Data that describes the qualities of something such as the color of the sky or the texture of a material.

Quantitative—Data that can be measured by quantity such as height, weight, and temperature.

Raspberry Pi—A series of small computers developed to promote computer science and computing in developing countries (https://www.raspberrypi.org).

Remind—A web system teachers use to notify students via text or email (https://www.remind.com).

Resnick, Mitch—LEGO Papert Professor of Learning Research and head of the Lifelong Kindergarten group at the MIT Media Lab (the group that developed Scratch and many other awesome projects).

Rigamajig—A large-scale building kit, including planks, pulleys, wheels, bolts, and nuts, designed for hands-on play and learning (http://rigamajig.com).

Rosenbaum, Eric—Co-inventor of Makey Makey, member of Lifelong Kindergarten group at MIT.

Rube Goldberg Machine—A contraption that has been deliberately overengineered to perform a simple task (https://www.rubegoldberg.com).

Scratch paper—Experiments in using the Arduino extension for Scratch and paper circuits.

Scratch programming—A free programming language that uses block coding. Also an online community for creating and sharing games and animations. Created by MIT students. (https://scratch.mit.edu).

ScratchX—Experimental extensions for Scratch programming.

Sewing circuits—Using conductive thread to sew LEDs to fabric.

Silver, Jay—Co-inventor of Makey Makey and member of Lifelong Kindergarten group at MIT.

SketchUp—3D modeling software (http://www.sketchup.com).

Skype—An application that allows users to instant message, voice call, or video call (https://www.skype.com/en).

Snap Circuits—An educational toy that allows children to create circuits by snapping pieces together (http://www.snapcircuits.net).

Socratic Seminar—A formal discussion based on a text where a leader asks open-ended questions.

Soldering—A process that joins two or more metal pieces together with solder and a soldering iron.

SoundCloud—Audio sharing social media website. Primarily music and podcasts (https://soundcloud.com).

SparkFun—An online electronics retail store that manufactures electronics and offers maker education for teachers (https://www.sparkfun.com).

Sphero—A Bluetooth-enabled robotic ball that can be controlled and programmed using a variety of apps (http://www.sphero.com/education).

STEAM—Science, technology, engineering, arts, and math.

STEM—Science, technology, engineering, and math.

Students Rebuild—Service projects geared toward young people (http://studentsrebuild.org).

Synth—An instrument that converts an electrical signal into sound.

Teaming table—A table with a computer monitor and a variety of connector cables that students can use to connect their devices, display their screens, and collaborate.

3D Printer—A machine that produces an item by building successive layers of a material such as plastic.

Tinkercad—A simple online 3D design and print tool (https://www.tinkercad .com).

Tinkering—The process of exploring, messing around, and experimenting with or without necessarily having a clear goal in mind.

The Tinkering Studio—A studio workshop located in the Exploratorium museum in San Francisco, California (http://tinkering.exploratorium.edu).

Trebuchet—A type of catapult that uses a counterweight to increase the distance an object is thrown.

Twitter—A social media microblogging site where all posts are 140 characters or less (https://twitter.com).

Videoconferencing—Using a video chat, such as Skype or Google Hangouts, to meet virtually with someone else.

Wilkinson, Karen—Director of The Tinkering Studio.

YouTube—A video-sharing social media website (https://www.youtube.com).

Index

About the Authors

COLLEEN GRAVES is a teacher librarian and creative education consultant. She is passionate about makerspaces as well as promoting a reading culture. Graves was awarded the Innovator award as a 2016 *Library Journal* Mover and Shaker and was a cofinalist for *School Library Journal*'s School Librarian of the Year in 2014. This is her third book written with her husband and fellow librarian, Aaron Graves. She actively documents her makerspace journey on her blog at colleengraves.org, on Twitter, and on Instagram.

AARON GRAVES is a school librarian with 18 years of experience in education. Equal parts book lover, robot geek, and tech wizard, Graves gained his perseverance for maker projects through collaborative and interactive art experiences as a member of the Good/Bad Art Collective. He is an active speaker and presenter on libraries, makerspaces, and research skills, and he spends his free time writing, restoring microcars, and inventing things that make people smile.

DIANA L. RENDINA, MLIS, was media specialist at Stewart Middle Magnet School in Tampa, Florida from 2010–2017. She is now the media specialist at Tampa Preparatory School. She is the creator of the RenovatedLearning.com blog and is also a monthly contributor to AASL Knowledge Quest. Rendina participates actively in the International Society for Technology in Education Librarians Network, the American Association of School Librarians, and the Florida Association for Media in Education. She served on the Sunshine State Young Readers Award Committee from 2012 to 2015. She is the winner of the 2015 ISTE Librarians Network Award, the 2015 AASL Frances Henne Award for emerging leaders, and the 2015 *School Library Journal* Build Something Bold Award. She has presented on the Maker Movement at state, national, and international conferences, including AASL, FETC, and ISTE. Diana shares resources regularly on Twitter, Pinterest, and Instagram @DianaLRendina.